Bob Nudd's
ILLUSTRATED GUIDE TO
Pole Fishing

Acknowledgements

The publishers would like to thank the following:
Iain Toombs of *Improve Your Coarse Fishing* magazine for putting together the 'Pole Clinic' series and Gareth Purnell of *Improve Your Coarse Fishing* for overseeing this book.

Photographers:
Fiona Spencer, Paul Marriott, Angus Murray and Mick Rouse. Malcolm Lane for the illustrations.

Finally a big thanks to:
Bob Nudd for working closely with the *Improve Your Coarse Fishing* team to reveal the pole-fishing techniques which have helped him to three individual world championship gold medals.

ISBN 0 9533087 1 5

Produced by
Publishing Promotions **PP**
1 High Street
Princes Risborough
Bucks HP27 0AG

Published by
Emap Pursuit Publishing Ltd
Bretton Court
Bretton
Peterborough PE3 8DZ

Bob Nudd's
ILLUSTRATED GUIDE TO
Pole Fishing

emap.

Contents

Introduction *Bob sets the scene* **6**

Your new pole *Buyer's guide and tips* **8**

Elastic and tension *Setting up a pole* **12**

Pole floats *The definitive guide* **16**

Making pole rigs *Rigging up Bob's way* **20**

Hook patterns *Hooks and attaching them* **24**

The perfect pole peg *Setting out your fishing spot* **28**

Every second counts *Best ways to set up your tackle* **34**

Find those fish *Groundbaiting* **40**

Don't just sit there! *Tactics on the river* **44**

World-class angler *A closer look at Bob's winning ways* **48**

Everything to play for *Rigs for catching carp* **52**

Liquid Gold *Loosefeeding for carp* **56**

Fast and furious *More on carp* **60**

Keep it up! *Carp feeding frenzy* **64**

Tipped for the top! *50 tips for the best catches* **68**

Q&A pole fishing browser *Your queries answered* **74**

Jargon Buster *Pole fishing terms explained* **92**

Introduction

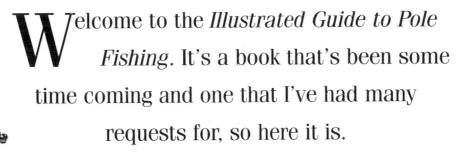

Welcome to the *Illustrated Guide to Pole Fishing*. It's a book that's been some time coming and one that I've had many requests for, so here it is.

I've compiled the pages from the best of my long-running 'Pole Clinic' series, a range of articles that was created to help all you pole anglers get the very best from your equipment.

In this book I've packed in as many hints, tips and as much general advice as possible, with just the one aim in mind – to give you the chance to match poles with the best anglers around, and best of all, to get those fish out of the water and into your keepnet!

Best of luck to you all.

Bob Nudd

Your new pole

W hether you're considering buying your first pole, already have one but are confused about how to get the most from it, or consider yourself an expert, you need Bob's expertise

Your first pole

Of all the considerations when buying your first pole, price is top of the pile. So it should be too, as poles, especially good ones, do not come cheap, with many costing well over the £1000 mark.

However, various manufacturers have at last started to react to real market needs and have drip-fed some excellent lower-priced poles onto the market.

Such examples as the Maver Jurassic Carp (14 metres for under £400), Drennan Series 2, the new Browning Synthetizor Plus, Shakespeare's Onset and Garbolino's Calibra and Rio offer tremendous value for money.

▲ *First, decide what sort of pole you need.*

But before heading off to your local tackle shop or diving head first into a mail order catalogue to snap up the cheapest on the market, you must determine what you want from your pole.

If you fish carp waters with fish to double figures, a slim finesse pole is not really the best of choices.

▲ *Check out a few in your tackle shop.*

If you never fish such waters there are stacks of poles on the market which are suitable for river, canal and stillwater fishing.

These competition or 'roach poles' are as stiff as possible in all but the top three sections, enabling the angler to achieve excellent presentation at distance, especially in a wind.

They tend to have a fast taper. This means each section decreases in diameter significantly and therefore minimises the overall weight and gives the pole a distinct 'tip action', ideal for playing smaller fish.

If you do all sorts of pole fishing, then an all-round pole will certainly be your best bet. These versions are stronger, have slightly thicker walls and are a little heavier than competition poles.

They also have a slightly more forgiving action, bending throughout the top few sections. Larger fish can be tackled confidently provided you do not exert too much pressure and the pole is equipped with the correct elastic and your rig balanced. I'll

be talking about these considerations later in the book.

If you are a regular 'carp cruncher', then you obviously need a specialist carp pole, as a finesse pole would snap under the strain of hauling away at big bags of hard-fighting carp.

The majority of carp poles are designed with a very slight taper which makes the tip sections much stronger and thicker walled making the whole pole quite heavy in comparison to competition poles.

They have an almost all-through action in which virtually the whole length bends to help cushion the surges of large, hard-fighting carp.

In the balance

OK, so you've decided what sort of pole you need, and you buy an angling mag like Improve to see what's on the market.

An eye-catching photograph and impressive blurb in a magazine or mail order catalogue may persuade you into thinking that you've found the pole for you. But don't jump in just yet.

No-one can ever get a true feel of what a

Three winning poles.

pole is like until they pick it up. Give your local tackle shop a ring, tell them what you have got in mind and see if they have a version in stock. If they haven't, most tackle shops will get the pole you wish within a few days for you to handle.

Don't pay too much attention to the weight printed on the pole until you've tried it either. Most are measured with the pole broken down and placed on a scale.

But when the actual pole is set-up and in use it may feel a lot heavier, or a lot lighter, than you expect.

This is all down to balance. Most manufacturers construct their poles using different methods throughout the length, therefore altering the pole's balance.

And a pole that feels perfect to one angler may feel all wrong to another. The secret is to try a few out

What's in a pole

Another major factor to bear in mind is the material used in the pole's construction. There are carbon, carbon composite and glass fibre poles to choose from.

▲ *Don't pay too much attention to weight...*   ▲ *Check for any manufacturing faults – you don't want to have to return the pole afterwards.*

Carbon is by far the strongest, lightest and stiffest material, but is expensive. Maver make one carbon pole with a price tag of £8000 and there are plenty in the £1500 to £3000 bracket.

Carbon composite poles are a little heavier, 'softer' in their action (they bend more) and more friendly on the pocket.

Glass fibre poles are by far the cheapest, but very strong. They tend to be soft and therefore 'droop' when used beyond five metres.

Most glass fibre poles on the market are telescopic throughout and are designed purely for whip fishing.

▲ *It's better to set up the pole outside the shop.*

Get a grip!

The next, and the most important stage is to put the pole together, either indoors or outdoors. All tackle shops will allow you to do this. With the pole at its full length you can get a true picture of its performance and whether it suits you.

Poles have put-in joints, where the lower, bigger section fits over the upper, or put-over joints, where the bigger section fits into the smaller.

Always pick up the next pole with an open mind no matter what the price tag (it's often best that you don't know it as this can cloud your judgement), as you could be pleasantly surprised. Here are my tips for finding the perfect pole for you:

• Forget the fancy look of the pole as this is not going to help you catch a fish. The pole's rigidity, weight and action are the important factors.

• Sit on a tackle box and add sections until you are holding the pole at its full extent. Politely ask a shop assistant to pull the pole tip to the ground. This will give you a good idea of the pole's action and how it will cope with hooked fish.

▶ *Selecting a pole is entirely a personal choice, as you're the one who will be using it.*

- Always check the condition of the pole. Lightly squeeze the walls of every section to search for weak spots or any manufacturing faults. The weak areas will be detectable as the pole section will bend inwards when pressure is applied. It's very rare that a pole will reach a tackle shop shelf with a fault but it occasionally happens.
- Finally, enquire about the cost of spare sections. If you intend on venturing onto the competition match circuit or if you take your pleasure fishing very seriously, you may need some extra 'top three kits' or even an extension in the future. They can cost more than you think.

The most important thing

Many anglers think that when you add an extension to your pole this will make it become almost unmanageable. This is often not the case. Many manufacturers design their poles at their fullest length, with the extensions attached.

The most important thing of all is that you must be happy with the way the pole feels to YOU before you hand over any loot.

Never forget that you are the one who'll be sitting holding the thing for hours on end and if you are not sure about the way it handles, in the first place, this will soon shine through after a few hours on the bank in a wind!

Above all, enjoy using it. Pole-fishing is a great method and without any question it gives better bait presentation than any other method if used correctly.

◀ *The new pole in action! Before choosing one, think what sort you need, decide on a maximum price, try several poles out before you buy, check every section and don't forget to ask the cost of spare sections. Note that it is possible to get great deals and discounts on the manufacturers' retail prices indicated in the box.*

BOB'S TOP FIVE BUDGET POLE CHOICE

POLE	LENGTH	WEIGHT	RRP PRICE	TOP KITS	EXTENSION
Maver Jurassic Carp	11m	850g	£299.00	Extra top three provided	£50.00
Drennan Series 2	11m	720g	£371.00	£53.75	£79.00
Browning Synthetizor Plus	11m	945g	£199	Extra top three provided	N/A
Garbolino Calibra	12.4m	1145g	£399	Extra top two kit provided	N/A
Shakespeare Onset	11m	996g	£150	Top 4 £49.99	£32.00

Elastic and tension

W ell, you've got your new pole; now it's time for Bob to reveal how he fits his elastic and gets perfect tension, each time, every time

I f you read the last chapter thoroughly, you will know exactly what to look out for when buying your first pole. If you have actually bought yourself a new pole by now, then congratulations.

The next and most critical stage is to make sure your pole is fitted with the correct elastic with the right amount of tension.

The elastic, and the way it's fitted, need to suit both the pole you are using, and the type of fish that you are targeting. For example, if you have just purchased a carp pole you would be absolutely crazy to rig it up with a light number three elastic through one section.

If you used that set-up, any self-respecting carp would bottom out the elastic in no time and you'd end up with either a snapped rig, or, if your main line was very strong, you'd be risking a snapped pole. Both fit firmly into the disaster category!

So, let's determine exactly what elastic you need to suit the fish you wish to catch.

Have a good look at the table (overleaf) and

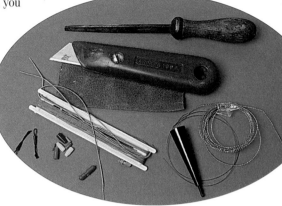

▲ *Tools for the job.*

study the comparisons between the various strengths of elastic and what they are best used for.

You will also be able to determine through how many sections you would be best threading your elastic.

So, if you wish to fish for good sized roach and small skimmer bream you would do best buying either number three or four elastic and it should be threaded through the pole's top two sections etc.

As a general rule of thumb, I usually fit really light elastics through just the top section, medium elastics through two sections, and heavy elastics through three.

The more sections you put your elastic through, the more elastic you have in your pole, therefore the more stretch you have.

For big fish like carp which are likely to set off on long powerful runs you usually need a lot of stretch to avoid being snapped and therefore an elastic through three sections is appropriate.

But you also need a strong elastic which will tire the fish out, otherwise you'd be playing a 4 lb plus fish for hours, so you need a thick elastic like a 12.

Threading tools

First of all, you need to have the right tools to do the job properly. To thread the elastic through the pole's sections you will need a diamond eye threader. This, like all the other items I mention here, can be bought fairly

cheaply in your local tackle shop.

Next, to protect the elastic from any sharp edges at the end of the pole you need to obtain a PTFE bush.

There are two styles on the market, one fits inside the pole tip, the other slides on the outside of the pole tip. The choice is yours, but to help you along I will explain the advantages of each version later.

You will also need a bung to lock the elastic in place at the end of your desired pole section.

For attaching your elastic to the rig mainline you will need a connector. The plastic Stonfo connector like the one pictured is the most popular on the market as it's really easy to use, but there are other ways of connecting your rig to the elastic as I'll explain later in the series.

And finally there are the tools for cutting your pole back. I prefer using a file, a version having a sharp edge is best, or failing that a sharp craft knife. Fine sandpaper will also come in useful, as will a tube of superglue.

▲ *Care and a good eye are two essentials for fitting elastic successfully.*

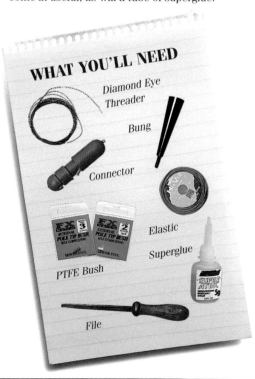

WHAT YOU'LL NEED

Diamond Eye Threader

Bung

Connector

Elastic

Superglue

PTFE Bush

File

Elasticating with an external PTFE bush

Whatever size elastic you use, make sure it slides through your PTFE bush easily. The smaller the gap between bush and elastic the better, but don't over-tighten or the elastic won't slide through. This tiny gap prevents dirt entering the pole, which can affect performance, cause abrasions and reduce the elastic's lifespan.

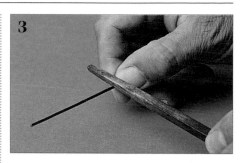

Cut the top section to fit the bush. I use a Seymo Metric Tip Gauge, which has 22 holes, all marked with their diameter. I look at the diameter on the bush packaging and find this on the gauge. I slip the gauge over the pole until it's tight and score a line on the pole. If you have no tip gauge, guess the diameter, score with a sharp object.

Carefully cut through the pole at the point you calculated or guessed. I use a sharp-edged file as it cuts smoothly. Alternatively you can use a craft knife. Turn the pole when cutting in order to achieve a perfect slice. I would recommend you cut a little less than you guessed as you can always make another cut if you're wrong.

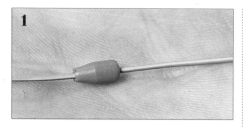

See if your bush fits snugly onto the end of your pole. If not, make another cut further along the pole's tip section and try again. When you have found the correct length and your bush is tight against the pole, sand the tip at right angles until it feels smooth. You can do this with a fine file or sandpaper placed on a flat surface.

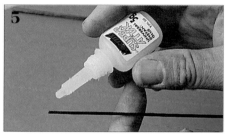

Carefully add a drop of superglue to the outside of your pole and gently push on the PTFE bush. Quickly remove any surplus glue which spreads onto your pole. Never do this by hand – a fast wipe with either a cloth or tissue will suffice. Leave for a minute or so and then check to see if the bush is stuck fast. Now the pole is complete.

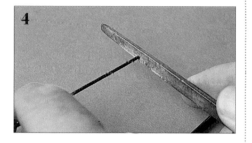

Push the bung into the last section to be elasticated and twist round. The pole's outer rim scores a line on the bung, telling you the section diameter. If your pole has a telescopic top three and you wish to elasticate one or two sections, cut the bung 1mm above the scored line. For three sections cut the bung 1mm below the line.

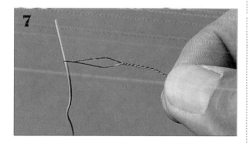

Now to elasticate the pole. Pass 10mm of elastic through the large eye of your diamond eye threader. Pull the elastic into the smaller eye and it will lock in place. Begin threading the wire, blunt end first, into the bush. Push the wire into the pole until it appears at the other end. Pull the elastic through the bush.

Once the elastic is through one, two or three sections remove the diamond eye threader. Pass the elastic through the bung's eye and form a 10-inch loop. Tie with a double overhand loop and wet the knot before pulling tight. Make sure there is something attached to the bottom of the bung which allows you to pull it out later.

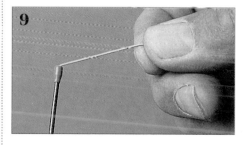

Make sure the sections to be elasticated are at their full length. Disconnect the connector sleeve and thread it, rounded end first onto the elastic. With fingers and thumb, gently pull the elastic to and from the pole tip until you find its returning point. The trick is to get the elastic to slip back gently, not snap back. Mark this point.

Thread on the connector and tie, on the returning point discovered in step 9 with a double overhand loop. As with all knots remember to wet it thoroughly before pulling tight and always make sure the knot is as tight to the plastic connector as possible, never leave a loop. It should now slide back into the pole.

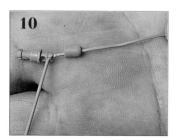

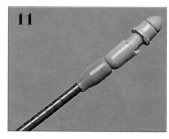

Push the sleeve onto the connector trapping the excess elastic. Cut the waste elastic close to the connector. This ensures the connector is doubly safe. When you let go of the connector it should slide smoothly back to the bush and stop. If elastic hangs out, tie the connector a little further down the elastic.

Elasticating with an internal PTFE brush

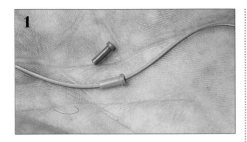

Again, select an internal PTFE bush which has a wide enough diameter to allow your elastic to slide through easily but not too wide so dirt will enter the inside of your pole.

Guess how much of the pole you need to cut so the bush sits snugly inside. Saw through the pole with the sharp edge of a file or a craft knife. Revolve the pole when cutting to get a straight edge. It's best to cut the pole shy of your estimation as you can always make another cut.

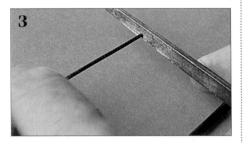

See if your bush fits into the end of your pole. If it does not, gently scrape the inside of the pole tip with the point of your knife using a circular motion. If this does not work cut the pole again an inch further along. When the correct length is found sand the pole tip until it feels smooth.

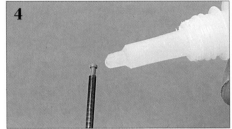

Add a drop of glue to your bush and push into the pole's tip to complete the top section. I prefer to sand the last two inches of pole with fine sandpaper. Follow steps 6-11 on the previous page to complete the process.

In the bushes

Now, back to the PTFE bushes. As I said, there are two versions, internal and external. I prefer to use internal bushes when possible as they are a lot neater. This is because they slip inside the tip section and therefore do not obstruct either line or your elastic. There's only one problem with this sort and that's having to cut the pole back quite far in order to fit the bush, especially when using thicker elastic. At worst this can cause as much as two feet in length to be lost from your pole.

External bushes, on the other hand, just slide over your tip section. This means that you will not have anywhere near as much carbon to cut off your pole to get the perfect fit. In putting on an external bush you will save almost two feet in length, and that can make a lot of difference, especially when you need to reach a far bank shelf or feature.

Externals are by far the best bush to use in conjunction with super strength elastics, as they tend to have a larger range of hole diameters.

I have found, however, two problems with this style of bush, the first of which can be quite disastrous if you continue to fish without noticing.

Firstly, because the bush sticks out from the side of the pole, the main line can become trapped around the bush when shipping your pole out, especially when using an ultra-light rig. If you hook a decent fish when this happens your elastic may not slip from the tip and all the force of the fish will be directed through the pole. This is definitely not something you want happening, especially if you've forked out hundreds of pounds only to see your pole smashed to smithereens!

Secondly, external bushes do not look as neat as internal bushes. They can cause your eye to be distracted from the pole float and you may miss bites. The choice is yours.

ELASTIC COMPARISON GUIDE			
ELASTIC	**NUMBER**	**FISH**	**SECTIONS**
FINE	1,2	Gudgeon, bleak, small perch, roach and skimmer bream	1
MEDIUM	3,4	Skimmer bream, hybrids, quality roach and small chub	2
STRONG	5,6	Bream, small tench, small carp, chub	2
VERY STRONG	8,9,10	Carp, tench, chub	3
SUPER	14+	Carp, barbel	3

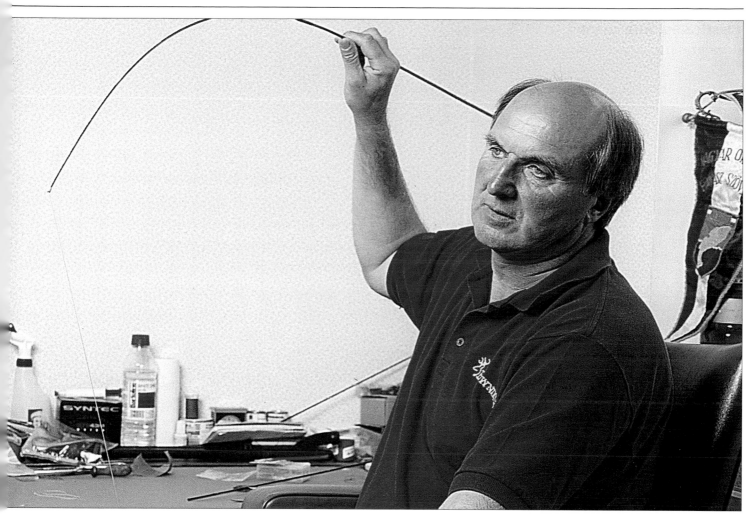

▲ Getting the right
tension can be a
painstaking job, but
it's all worthwhile
when you get to land
that dream fish.

◄ Correct elastic and
tension is a vitally
important part of
getting those fish out
of the water.

Pole floats

There are so many models of pole float available that choosing the right one can be a big headache – but not any more! Here's the definitive guide on everything you ever needed to know about pole floats

Dibber

Venues Suitable for canal or stillwater.

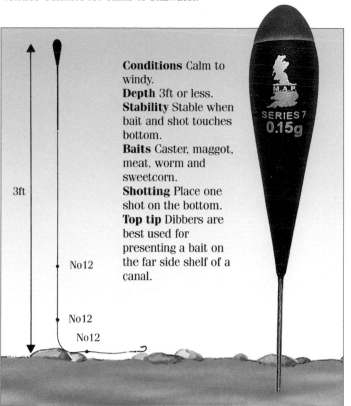

Conditions Calm to windy.
Depth 3ft or less.
Stability Stable when bait and shot touches bottom.
Baits Caster, maggot, meat, worm and sweetcorn.
Shotting Place one shot on the bottom.
Top tip Dibbers are best used for presenting a bait on the far side shelf of a canal.

3ft

No12

No12
No12

Straight

Venues Suitable for shallow stillwaters.

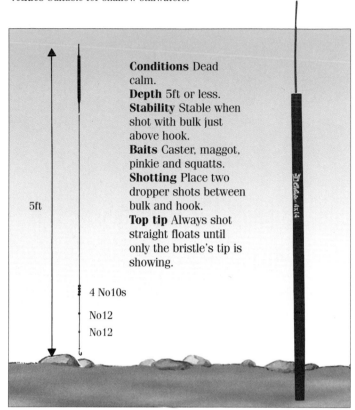

Conditions Dead calm.
Depth 5ft or less.
Stability Stable when shot with bulk just above hook.
Baits Caster, maggot, pinkie and squatts.
Shotting Place two dropper shots between bulk and hook.
Top tip Always shot straight floats until only the bristle's tip is showing.

5ft

4 No10s

No12

No12

Slim

Venues Suitable for canal, drain, stillwater or sluggish river.

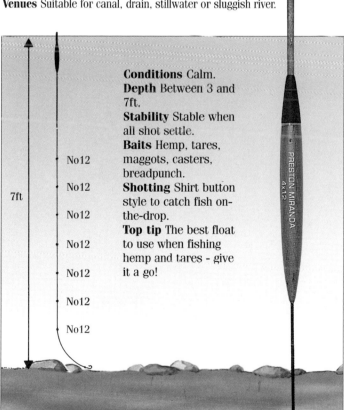

Conditions Calm.
Depth Between 3 and 7ft.
Stability Stable when all shot settle.
Baits Hemp, tares, maggots, casters, breadpunch.
Shotting Shirt button style to catch fish on-the-drop.
Top tip The best float to use when fishing hemp and tares - give it a go!

7ft

No12
No12
No12
No12
No12
No12
No12

Pear

Venues Suitable for canal, drain and stillwater.

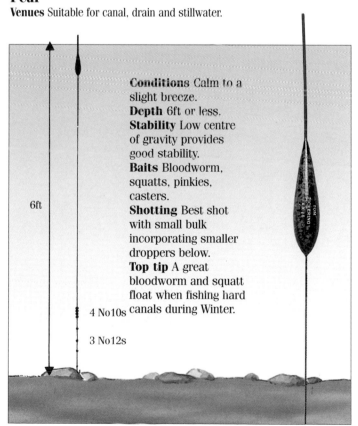

Conditions Calm to a slight breeze.
Depth 6ft or less.
Stability Low centre of gravity provides good stability.
Baits Bloodworm, squatts, pinkies, casters.
Shotting Best shot with small bulk incorporating smaller droppers below.
Top tip A great bloodworm and squatt float when fishing hard canals during Winter.

6ft

4 No10s

3 No12s

Body-up
Venue Suitable for deep rivers.

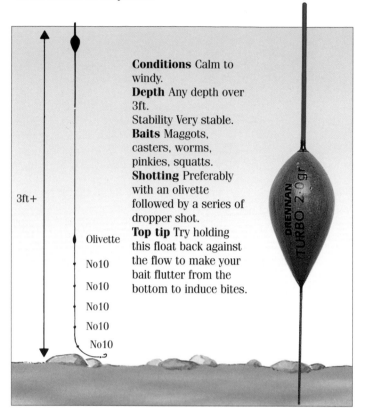

Conditions Calm to windy.
Depth Any depth over 3ft.
Stability Very stable.
Baits Maggots, casters, worms, pinkies, squatts.
Shotting Preferably with an olivette followed by a series of dropper shot.
Top tip Try holding this float back against the flow to make your bait flutter from the bottom to induce bites.

3ft+
Olivette
No10
No10
No10
No10
No10

Body-down
Venue Suitable for deep stillwaters.

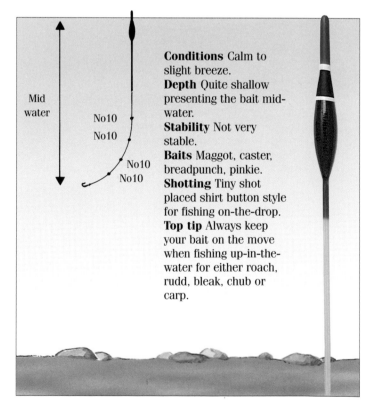

Conditions Calm to windy.
Depth Any depth over 6ft.
Stability Low centre of gravity provides great stability.
Baits Casters, maggots, meat, worms, sweetcorn, pastes.
Shotting With an olivette coupled with a series of tiny dropper shot below.
Top tip Have at least 6in of line overdepth with the final dropper shot placed 2in off the bottom.

6ft+
Olivette
No10
No10

Round
Venue Suitable for river or stillwater.

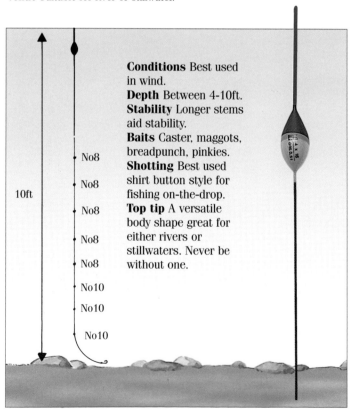

Conditions Best used in wind.
Depth Between 4-10ft.
Stability Longer stems aid stability.
Baits Caster, maggots, breadpunch, pinkies.
Shotting Best used shirt button style for fishing on-the-drop.
Top tip A versatile body shape great for either rivers or stillwaters. Never be without one.

10ft
No8
No8
No8
No8
No8
No10
No10
No10

Shallow
Venue Suitable for sluggish rivers, canals or stillwaters.

Conditions Calm to slight breeze.
Depth Quite shallow presenting the bait mid-water.
Stability Not very stable.
Baits Maggot, caster, breadpunch, pinkie.
Shotting Tiny shot placed shirt button style for fishing on-the-drop.
Top tip Always keep your bait on the move when fishing up-in-the-water for either roach, rudd, bleak, chub or carp.

Mid water
No10
No10
No10
No10

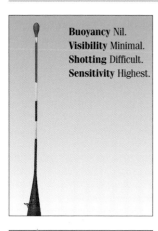

Buoyancy Nil.
Visibility Minimal.
Shotting Difficult.
Sensitivity Highest.

Wire

Unless fish in your local venue are really shy-biting try to avoid wire bristled floats as much as possible - they are a real headache to set-up. Once the float body has been shot even a tiny No13 will sink the bristle! They are extremely thin and difficult to see at distances. Many anglers add some grease to wire bristles to make them both more visible and buoyant. They are the most sensitive of all float bristles and register the tiniest of bites. Best used when presenting a tiny bait like squatts or bloodworm on the bottom under a bulk of shot.

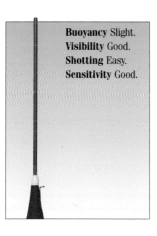

Buoyancy Nil.
Visibility Minimal.
Shotting Difficult.
Sensitivity High.

Carbon

Carbon bristles have similar properties to wire bristles. They sink, so shotting poses problems and is best left to the more experienced angler. They are a continuation of the carbon stem and are the same thickness plus a layer of paint. To make one stand out, paint it white, then re-coat with a fluorescent colour. To stop the bristle being dragged under, smear vaseline over the bristle. As carbon bristles aren't buoyant do not use large baits: stick to maggots, casters, squatts or pinkies.

Buoyancy Slight.
Visibility Good.
Shotting Easy.
Sensitivity Good.

Nylon

Nylon bristles are the popular choice for both anglers and manufacturers. They are readily available, cheap and are not brittle like carbon or cane stems. There's a wide choice of colours and thicknesses depending upon distance to be fished and eyesight quality. They are slightly buoyant so shotting is easier than wire and carbon versions. It may take three No12 shot to sink a long nylon bristle so they can be dotted right down for extra sensitivity. Their slightly buoyant properties allow heavier baits such as meat or worms to be used on the hook.

Buoyancy High.
Visibility Good.
Shotting Easy.
Sensitivity Fair.

Cane

These bristles, generally being quite thick, are fairly buoyant and allow heavy baits such as meat, worms or sweetcorn to be presented just off the bottom without dragging the float under. Cane bristles are best when selecting a float for fishing on the drop because the bristle can register each shot settling. Another plus point is that the bristles are generally thicker and more visible than other types. This doesn't hinder the float's sensitivity as you can dot the float right down. Best shot with a bulk incorporating three smaller shot under.

Stability The extra weight provides good stability.
Length Often very long compared to the float body.
Strength By far the strongest of all stems.
Diameter Very thin and fine.

Wire

Wire stems are by far the best ones to use when fishing a large bulk of shot or an olivette placed near to the hook. The longer the wire stem the less shot required down the line as the weight of the wire itself cocks the float. Select a wire stemmed float when fishing in windy conditions on either a river or stillwater as the wire's weight pulling on the float body adds extra stability to your rig.

Stability Offers a little less stability than wire stems.
Length Often quite long to aid stability.
Strength Strong, flexible but brittle.
Diameter Averaging twice the diameter of wire.

Carbon

Carbon offers similar properties to that of wire stemmed floats except carbon is a little lighter and more versatile. With this in mind you can use bulk shot or an olivette with confidence. Also they can be used with an on-the-drop shotting pattern allowing the stem to cock with each settling shot. Carbon stems 'cast' well and therefore make good whip floats.

Stability Offers no stability at all.
Length Quite short compared to the float body.
Strength High in strength and very flexible.
Diameter The largest diameter of all pole floats.

Nylon

If you're fishing an on-the-drop pattern shirt button style down your mainline this is the stem for you. As the rig hits the water the float will lie flat and gradually tilt as each shot settles. If the float darts under or doesn't settle as it should, you have a bite. Nylon stems are very flexible and are difficult to break. A very lightweight stem that's great for both pole and whip fishing.

Stability Offers very little stability.
Length Very short stumpy stems.
Strength Very strong with little flexibility.
Diameter Mostly quite thick requiring wide silicone tubing.

Cane

Cane is widely used both for pole and whip set-ups. It sinks very slowly and when used with shot placed shirt button style it tilts gradually into place with each shot settling. Cane is a great material for fishing on-the-drop and is strong, stiff and yet slightly flexible. Try to avoid using cane stemmed floats in strong wind or on venues having strong currents as they aren't stable at all.

Making pole rigs

Making your own pole rigs is an enjoyable and rewarding process – especially when you catch fish on them. Here's everything you ever needed to know about rigging them up yourself

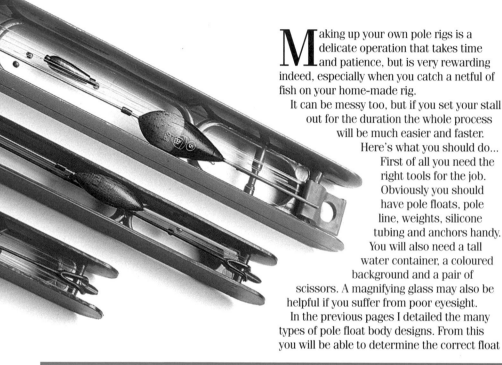

Making up your own pole rigs is a delicate operation that takes time and patience, but is very rewarding indeed, especially when you catch a netful of fish on your home-made rig.

It can be messy too, but if you set your stall out for the duration the whole process will be much easier and faster. Here's what you should do...

First of all you need the right tools for the job. Obviously you should have pole floats, pole line, weights, silicone tubing and anchors handy. You will also need a tall water container, a coloured background and a pair of scissors. A magnifying glass may also be helpful if you suffer from poor eyesight.

In the previous pages I detailed the many types of pole float body designs. From this you will be able to determine the correct float for the venue you are going to fish. The next major item you need to concentrate on is your line. There are two types available on the market nowadays. There is normal reel line such as Bayer Perlon, Maxima and Drennan Float Fish for example, and there's the very advanced high-tech pole line, such as Browning Cenitan XC, Pro Micron and Zeus, to name but three. And this is the line you should be using.

High-tech lines

The reason for this is because high-tech lines have a very low diameter but still retain a high breaking strain. This is because they are normally pre-stretched during the manufacturing process. As an example 2.1lb breaking strain Drennan Float Fish has a line diameter of 0.14mm and also plenty of stretch. A high-tech pole line having the same diameter, 0.14mm, will have a breaking strain in the region of 4lb, that's almost twice as much as normal reel line. With this in mind

EQUIPMENT THAT YOU NEED TO MAKE THE PERFECT POLE RIG

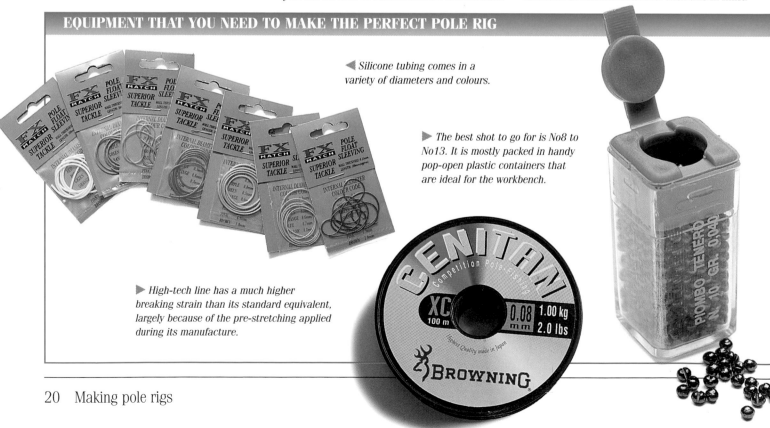

◀ Silicone tubing comes in a variety of diameters and colours.

▶ The best shot to go for is No8 to No13. It is mostly packed in handy pop-open plastic containers that are ideal for the workbench.

▶ High-tech line has a much higher breaking strain than its standard equivalent, largely because of the pre-stretching applied during its manufacture.

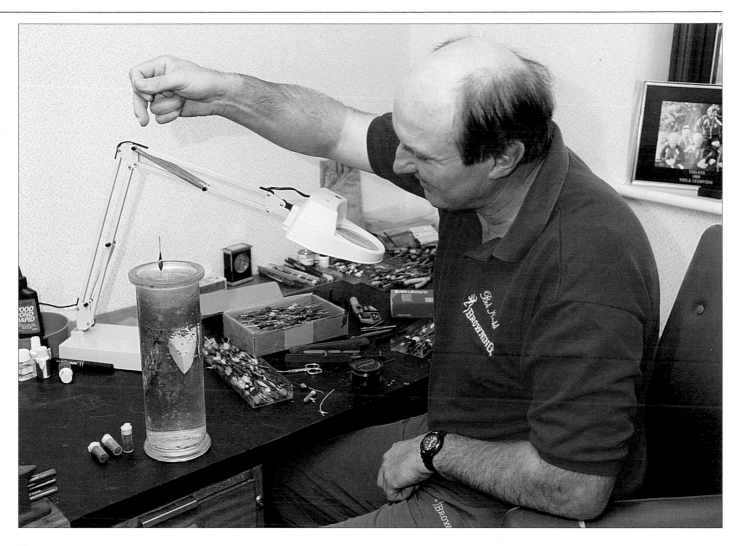

▲ Here Bob drops his latest float into a container to check how it sits in the water. The bristle should be just visible above the surface.

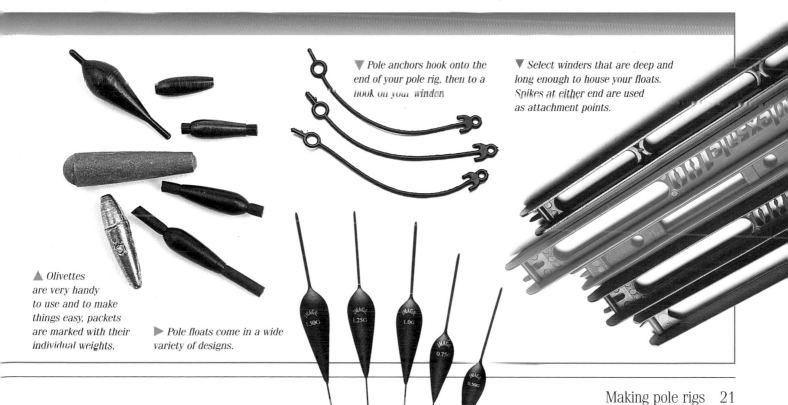

▼ Pole anchors hook onto the end of your pole rig, then to a hook on your winder.

▼ Select winders that are deep and long enough to house your floats. Spikes at either end are used as attachment points.

▲ Olivettes are very handy to use and to make things easy, packets are marked with their individual weights.

▶ Pole floats come in a wide variety of designs.

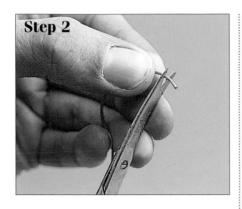

Step 2

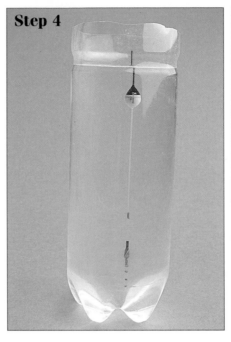

Step 4

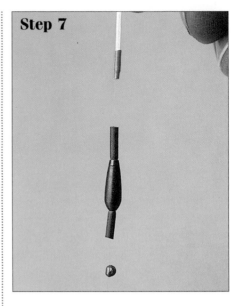

Step 7

Step 1

First thing's first - get your stall set out, with everything you need in front of you. It may be best to use a coloured background to help see the fine diameter line, small shot and silicone tubing. Fill your container almost to the brim with water and you're all set to go. Rigging pole floats is a very intricate and delicate operation. If you suffer from poor eyesight why not invest in a free-standing magnifying glass? It will make the whole process a lot clearer.

Step 2

Cut three small strips of silicone, each around 1cm long, and save two of these for later. Now cut off about eight to 10 inches of line. Thread this line through one of the silicone tubes and then push the silicone over the end of the pole float's stem. Now your line will be trapped securely against the float's stem.

Step 3

Now it's time to begin shotting the float. If you are due to fish a shallow venue and you wish your hookbait to fall through the water

slowly you must use a quantity of tiny shot like No11, 12 or 13. If you need your bait to get down to the bottom quickly you must use a bulk of larger shot such as No10 or, more favourably, you can use a neat olivette coupled with extra 'dust' shot to set the float correctly.

Step 4

Thread on your olivette, or squeeze shot, onto the line hanging from your pole float. Carefully drop the float into the water container to see how the float sits in the water. It will undoubtedly not settle right so retrieve the float and add or subtract more weight until the float settles correctly.

Ideally the float's bristle should

just be visible above the water surface. Always jot down or remember exactly what quantity and size of shot and/or olivette you have placed on the line.

Step 5

Gently slide the line and silicone from the float and leave to one side. Unravel about two feet of high-tech pole line from the spool (do not cut) and thread on your three short lengths of silicone. Now thread the end of your line through the float's tiny eye located near to the float's bristle. Push the float around two feet from the end of your line and push the three silicone tubes over the float stem locking the float in place. One should be pushed tight to the float body, one in the middle of the stem and the other should be right at the stem's tip, preferably hanging off by about 3 or 4mm.

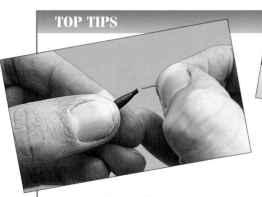

If you use olivettes threaded on the line, instead of locking them in place with shot, why not use an old float bristle? This prevents your olivette rubbing against line.

Mark on the winder all your rig's details. Use a sticky label for float weight, line length and diameter. Write on with a marker if you don't like labels.

Another useful tip is never to crush shot onto your line, as it will damage your rig. Just squeeze it on, as you will be able to move it and down the line, as required.

you can fish heavier breaking strain lines than you would with a rod and reel set-up and at the same time have a lower line diameter and therefore gain more bites as you aren't spooking fish.

Basic beginner's collection

A basic beginner's line collection should consist of 0.08mm, 0.10mm and 0.12mm spools. If you intend to go fishing for big carp you will need to get yourself some 0.14mm diameter line as well.

The next item you need are weights. You should forget about your SSGs, AAs and BBs, instead think along the lines of No8 to No13 shot. Also olivettes are handy, too, and are easy to use, as each packet of olivettes is marked with the individual weights. These

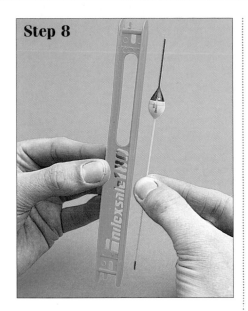

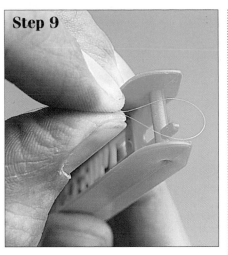

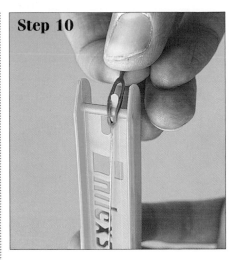

Step 6

Now tie a small loop in the end of your pole line above the float using a double overhand knot, remembering to dampen the knot before pulling tight. This will be used to attach the rig to your pole connector and to your anchors. Now unravel the length of line you will be requiring. If you are due to fish a five metre deep venue I would definitely advise that you rig the float with anything up to 6.5 metres of line, just in case water levels vary, you need to present a foot of line on the bottom or when fishing running water and you need to trot your float through the swim.

Step 7

If you are using an olivette either thread it, or attach it with silicone, onto the mainline. Then squeeze on the same size and amount

of shot you used when you originally tested the float in your water container. These should all be attached close to the end of your line. Now gently slide the shot up the line into the position you wish. Cut off the line which was crushed when you originally attached your shot as this is damaged and useless.

Step 8

Tie, using another overhand knot, a small loop in the end of your rig line. This completes the most intricate part of the rig making process. Now it's time to store the rig carefully on a winder.

Step 9

Select a winder deep and long enough to house your float. Most winders have two spikes located at either end. To one of these spikes clip on the loop closest to the shot. Begin winding the line under tension around your winder.

Step 10

When you reach the pole float you may have to slide it along the line to enable the float body to rest within the winder's groove. Continue winding on the line until you reach the end loop. Finally, attach an anchor with its end clip and stretch to attach to the winder's second spike.

Hey Presto! Your first home-made rig!

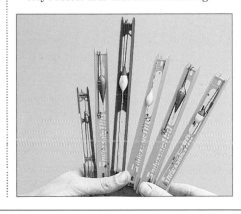

provide a neat bulk weight that will get your bait down to the bottom in no time at all. The other option is to use styles. A style is a cylindrical weight which clasps onto the line. Unfortunately styles lock solid when in place and therefore cannot be slid up and down the line to alter shotting patterns. With this in mind it is probably best avoiding styles as much as possible.

To attach your float to the line you will need a selection of fine diameter silicone tubing. Coloured versions are better to use as you can see them much more easily when you work on your rigs.

Pole anchors

Pole anchors are a vital item, too. They simply hook onto the end of your pole rig and

then to a hook on your winder. This keeps the rig under tension and secure on your winder.

Selecting anchors

When selecting anchors, go for the ones with plenty of stretch, as they will not damage your line when placed under tension for long periods of time.

You will also need a water container of some sort. I use a large glass bottle, but an old plastic lemonade bottle with the top cut off will do fine. When almost full with water you can place your float in the water to see if it's shot correctly.

▼ *Make up two of each rig. Then, if you get in a tangle, you can easily detach the first rig and clip on your spare.*

Hook patterns

If you were to choose the right pattern hook to match your bait or the correct mainline for your pole elastic would you get it right every time? Read on, and soon, you'll be doing it as well as the triple world champion

There are many hook patterns available to today's angler – so many, in fact, that choosing the right one for your chosen bait and method can be a real headache. There are short shank, long shank, wide gape, fine, medium and heavy gauge, round bend, crystal bend... the list can really go on and on.

So what are the factors that go into making a good hook? Which pattern is the right one to accompany the bait you are using for your session? Does the colour of the hook make a great deal of difference? What on earth is a crystal bend? Well, fear not. Here are all the answers.

To start with you need to match the hook to the shape of your chosen bait. I would never use the same hook pattern for both my hemp fishing and bloodworm work, for example.

Hook and wire

The strength of the hook and diameter of the wire used in its construction plays a very important role, too. There is no way that I would consider forcing a large, thick diameter forged hook through a tiny squatt or a pinkie, but I would consider using one when paste fishing for carp.

So allow me to detail exactly what style and pattern of hook I would use for the main eight coarse fishing baits and why I would do so. Bear in mind that I always use Browning hooks, as they are my sponsors, but I also provide some alternatives which can do much the same job.

◀ Hooks come in a galaxy of patterns. Here is just a small selection of the types on offer.

MAGGOT

I always use size 20 or 22 Browning Maggot hooks for this bait. This size matches the proportions of a maggot perfectly although I may step up to a size 18 or even a 16 if the fish are really having the bait. The hook has a fine wire and a tiny barb which prevents the maggot being burst when thread onto the hook and also allows it to wriggle attractively. The hook has a long point, short shank and crystal bend. This particular bend forces the wriggling maggot to lie directly below the hook point. Now the bait and point are directly in line and therefore produce more hooked fish on the strike.

Alternatives: Kamasan B520, Image IM6 Maggot, Tubertini Series 2.

CASTER

Caster proportions are very similar to those of a maggot so I would again use Browning Maggot hooks. When hooking casters through the side with the point protruding I go for size 20 and 22. If bites are at a premium or the fish are very wary I will bury the hook right inside the caster. If this is the case I would step up to a size 16 or 18 hook as the whole lot will be buried inside the bait. Again, the pattern of the Browning Maggot provides more hooked fish on the strike. As the hook's point is parallel with the shank it stands well proud of the caster's curved sides when hooked and therefore prevents missed bites on the strike.

Alternatives: Drennan Carbon Caster, Kamasan B611, Image IM5 Caster.

HEMP

Hemp is a solid circular seed which requires a special type of hook to ensure the point is set well away from the seed itself. I generally use a size 20 Browning Chikara Hemp hook but if the fish are going mad I might step up to an 18 or even 16. I always hook hemp by squeezing the grain to open it up, then I slip the hook shank into the gap and let go, so that the hemp clasps the hook tightly. Good hemp hooks have a medium shank length coupled with a wide gape. The short shank is completely hidden by the grain whereas the point protrudes from the shell enough to provide ample penetration.

Alternatives: Kamasan B511, Tubertini Series 0, Polemaster wide gape.

WORMS

I am most confident using the Browning Tournament Red in sizes 18 or 20. The colour gives me confidence as it is camouflaged against the worm's body. I break a small worm in half and thread it up the long hook shank. This disguises most of the hook while still leaving the point showing for extra penetration. Its crystal bend prevents the worm from wriggling off the hook. The point is straight and parallel with the shank. This provides me with the all important match-winning penetration I need. Hooks for chopped worm fishing must hold their sharpness well against a perch's hard mouth.

Alternatives: Drennan Team England Maggot, Kamasan B525.

PASTE

The only time I use paste is when I'm carp fishing and so a large strong hook is the order of the day. It really doesn't matter what size hook you use as the paste will be moulded around the metal disguising it from the fish. I prefer using Browning spade end Specimen hooks in sizes from 10 to 14. They are forged and therefore very strong and feature an inwardly curved point. This provides great holding power when playing fish. The Browning Specimen hook's wide gape and short shank is perfect for moulding paste onto and they also break free from soft paste balls with ease giving a clean crisp hold on fish.

Alternatives: Drennan Team England Barbless, Carbon Chub, Preston Pro Carp.

BREAD

Fishing punched bread is an artform which requires the right hook. I choose small lightweight hooks which won't force the bait through the water too quickly when fishing on-the-drop. I use either size 18 or 20 Browning Breadpunch hook which is constructed from fine wire, has a long shank and a slightly curved-in point. As soon as the hooked bread hits the water it expands concealing most of the shank. I'm not too fussed about the remainder showing as the silver hook almost matches the white bread. The curved-in point helps to retrieve the bread from the punch as well as providing a good hold on fish.

Alternatives: Tubertini Series 2, Image Bread Punch, Kamasan B511.

BLOODWORM

Bloodworm fishing requires the finest of all hooks. The bait has an extremely soft skin which bursts easily when hooking. With this in mind you need an ultra-fine hook with a tiny barb. I use size 26 to 20 Browning Bloodworm hooks. They have a very long shank, a slight crystal bend which provides a better strength to wire diameter and there's also a choice of barbless or barbed versions. It's always better to start the session on a small hook, but the fish often get so excited by all the loosefed joker they totally forget about the hook enabling me to step up to say, a size 20.

Alternatives: Preston Innovations Bloodworm Extra, Prism Seven Bloodworm Kamasan B512, Tubertini Series 1.

PINKIE AND SQUAT

For this bait I simply use a smaller version of the same hook I would adopt whenever big maggot fishing, namely the Browning Maggot. I prefer using size 22 to 24 hooks for pinkies and size 24 or 26 for squatts. In the smaller sizes these hooks have an incredibly fine wire gauge and so don't 'pop' the bait when inserting the hook.

As before, the crystal bend ensures both the pinkies and squatts do not wriggle off the hook and position them in such a way that you hardly ever miss bites. The tiny barb passes through the skin with ease.

If I do have any problems I press the barb down gently with a pair of pliers.

Alternatives: Preston Innovations Pinkie/Squatt, Drennan Polemaster, Kamasan B511.

BOB'S COMBINATIONS				
ELASTIC	MAINLINE	B/S	HOOKLENGTH	B/S
No1	0.09mm	2.3lb	0.06mm	1.1lb
No2	0.09mm	2.3lb	0.07mm	1.3lb
No3	0.10mm	2.5lb	0.08mm	2lb
No4	0.10mm	2.5lb	0.09mm	2.3lb
No5/6	0.12mm	3lb	0.10mm	2.5lb
No8/10	0.13mm	3.5lb	0.12mm	3lb
No12+	0.15mm	4.5lb	0.13mm	3.5lb

Now that the fog has been cleared away where hooks are concerned, my next task is to shine a little light on the correct use of low diameter high-tech pole fishing hooklengths.

There are many varying thicknesses available, from as little as 0.05mm diameter to as high as 0.15mm. As I've stated before they are very strong for their ultra-fine diameter, sometimes double the strength of ordinary monofilament, and hence the fish don't feel the line until it's too late.

The main problem with this high-tech line is choosing the right one for the style of fishing you intend doing. You will already have elasticated your pole, but now you must match the pole line to the elastic accordingly.

This is the most important part of the selection process. Obviously you must select a line to match the species you are targeting. For example, you shouldn't use a line having a diameter and breaking strain of say, 0.07mm and 1.3lb when carp fishing with No12 elastic. In this situation the line will simply snap within seconds of hooking a fish as the elastic is much too powerful for the frail line you are using.

At the bottom left is a simple table, which shows the elastic, mainline and hooklength combinations I most often use when pole fishing. If you follow these guidelines closely you will ensure that your elastic performs as it should, your line is not put under too much pressure. This way you can reckon on landing the vast majority of fish you hook.

Reliability

By far the most reliable method I've found to tie my hooklength to mainline is by using the loop-to-loop method (pictured in the

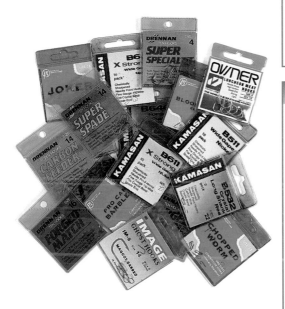

diagrams at top right on this page). I use this technique for nearly all my fishing, from roach and perch to tench and carp. It's really simple to do, and if you carefully follow the four easy steps shown here, you shouldn't go wrong.

Another method I employ when fishing really sensitive rigs in conjunction with blood worm and joker is to use a simple four-turn water knot (shown in the four step-by-step diagrams at right). In fact, this knot is not quite as strong as the loop-to-loop method, but it does provide a much neater link, which I much prefer when I am fishing ultra-fine.

ATTACHING HOOKLENGTH TO MAINLINE - METHOD 1

1
Form a loop in the end of your mainline and hold with finger and thumb. Hold the very end of this loop with your other hand. Form a second loop in the doubled-up line. Pass first loop through second loop twice.

2
Wet thoroughly and pull tight. Cut off excess line as close as you can to the knot and repeat the process with your hooklength. Try to form as small a loop as possible in both your lines in order to form a neat link.

3
Hold your mainline loop in your right hand and hold steady. With your left hand pass the hooklength loop over your mainline loop.

4
Push the loop up the main line and pass the hook through the main line loop. Pull tight to lock both lines together. Make sure no line is trapped behind the two knots formed in step 2.

ATTACHING HOOKLENGTH TO MAINLINE - METHOD 2

1
Lay both your hooklength and mainline together and form a large loop with the two of them.

2
Pass the end of both your mainline and hooklength through the loop formed in step one above.

3
Repeat this process until you have threaded the line through four times in total.

4
Wet the knot and pull tight gently. Cut off the excess line as close as possible to the knot.

The perfect pole peg

There's a lot more to setting your stall out than meets the eye.
Here are a few handy hints and tips on how a
triple world champion does it

You never stop learning in this game. Even now I pick up new techniques and methods which will either improve my fishing or make catching fish easier and smoother.

One of the most important things I have learned over the years is to set my stall out correctly. Everything should be close to hand, safely positioned and well organised. This ensures you fish well, are comfortable and more importantly, don't suffer from continuous backache. Read on and you too could will be making the most of every session you fish.

Easing the load
Those of you with a vast amount of tackle will know how heavy a fully ladened holdall, carryall and seatbox feels. Even short walks to your swim can be really hard work, leaving you breathless. One way to ease the pressure on your shoulders is to distribute the weight equally around your body.

Never pass straps over your neck. Running down the left side of your neck is the pulmonary artery. This passes oxygenated blood from your heart, to your brain and then back to your lungs. Extreme pressure applied directly onto this artery by the strap of your heavy box or carryall will constrict the flow. This causes problems, even on short walks. You may feel light-headed, faint, or when you remove your kit the rush of blood may cause violent nose-bleeds. This is the last thing you want when you're just about to start a session!

To alleviate this problem simply place both straps directly on top of each shoulder. For example, if I'm carrying my box on my left side, the strap is over my left shoulder and if my carryall is on the right, its strap is over

▲ *Off to the pole peg, kit packed and ready!*

the right shoulder. This balances out the two heaviest items; all that remains to worry about is your holdall.

I always place my holdall in front of my body. This does not affect the overall balance, and it's comfortable, too. I position the holdall strap over my neck until it lays across

my shoulder muscles. This ensures that the strap is kept away from the main artery. With your kit in this position you can walk long distances with ease.

Avoiding back pain
Many pole anglers suffer with terrible back pains, especially during cold weather. Luckily, I don't, and I put this down to the way I sit. I always ensure my seat and footplate are positioned in such a way that the top of my legs are dead level. Having a box with adjustable legs and footplate helps enormously. I would never be without my footplate now. Even the worst banks can be levelled out ensuring you fish in comfort.

I adjust the legs incorporated into my seatbox first. When the box sits level I pull out my footplate and adjust until it too is straight to the horizon. Then, when I sit on the box my thighs are level, my feet are flat to the footplate and I'm comfortable. This pays dividends, especially when pole fishing for any length of time. I always rest my pole on my right thigh with my right forearm pressing down onto it firmly. As stated before, my thigh is level to the ground and therefore, so is my pole.

Pole roller facts
Pole rollers are invaluable too. They allow you to ship-out and un-ship your pole quickly and smoothly. There are many models available today, from free-standing versions having integral legs to ones needing banksticks for support. I prefer a free-standing version as the set of four adjustable legs allows me to position the roller wherever I wish on solid ground.

The position of the roller is all-important too. Many questions sent to me concern this,

so it's about time I spread some light on it.

I see many anglers on the bankside with their pole rollers positioned too far away, or too close to the seated angler. This causes problems, especially when shipping out. The perfect place is easy to find, just follow these simple steps.

Setting up your pole

Set your pole up to the length you are fishing. Now find its balancing point, where the part in front of you is as heavy as the part behind you. Your roller should be positioned at the end of your pole - it's as simple as that!

Now, when your pole comes off the roller it remains parallel to the ground and makes the whole pole fishing process easy and smooth.

The position of your keepnet is crucial too. If it's too far away you may have to carry fish over to the net, ultimately wasting time.

▲ *Angle your keepnet upwards, so that you can use it as a pole rest. The entrance is best set at an angle of around 45 degrees.*

▲ *Bob Nudd never has back problems, and you can see why by looking carefully at the dotted lines. Note how his arms, thighs and feet are all parallel to the ground, with adjustments made with the footplate and feet on the box.*

I always place my keepnet at my feet. I can unhook the fish over the net and place them inside in one smooth simple operation. I would curse myself if I lost a fish in a match, as it could be the one that makes the difference between winning and losing.

My keepnet also has a dual purpose - it prevents my pole from slipping into the water. I adjust the net so the entrance is set at an angle of around 45 degrees. When I've unshipped I can then tuck the end of my pole into the net. Now I can proceed to unhook fish, re-bait the hook or alter my rig depth confident that my pole is safe and sound.

▲ *Wrong! The roller is too close to the angler and overbalances forwards.*

▲ *Wrong! This time the roller is too far away and it tips backwards.*

▲ *Correct! The pole comes off the roller and stays horizontal.*

This could be you, at ease and ready for some successful fishing! Having lugged all that hefty pole fishing kit from home, if you set up like Bob, this will give you the best chance at bagging that match-winning haul of fish. Note that here in Britain, keeping yourself warm while sitting for long periods is a big priority for much of the year – so, apart from making sure you have good, windproof clothes and hat, the warmth-factor includes a thermos of hot drink and supply of energy foods.

Keep your spare equipment neatly behind you. If you need a drink, something to eat or an item of tackle equipment you don't need to get off your seat to get it.

Get to grips with groundbait. If you are fishing a venue which requires small nuggets of groundbait to be introduced at regular intervals, place your mixing bowl close-by. You can mould small balls with one hand while still watching your float.

Buy yourself a footplate or a platform. Their legs can be positioned independently, smoothing out even the roughest of bank-sides. They allow your feet to be positioned flat and your thighs to be parallel to the water.

Put plenty of clothing layers on. A comfortable and warm angler will fish a lot better than a cold, miserable one. Also, don't forget to wear your your hat on all but warm days. Most body heat is lost straight up, off the top of your head, so keep it covered at all times.

Use a rig rest. These simple roosts are perfect for keeping your extra top kits off the ground and out of harm's way. I always keep my rig rest quite low in order to stop my top kits blowing around too much in strong winds. They are very cheap, at around £5.00, and are worth every penny.

Get yourself a baitwaiter. These simple, lightweight accessories allow your bait to be positioned directly alongside your seat. You'll no longer have to bend down to get your loosefeed, and with a little practice you'll be able to load your catapult without taking your eyes off the float.

Keep your landing net close at hand. I use my right hand to hold my pole and left hand to hold the landing net, so it makes sense to have the landing net positioned on my left. I need not overstretch to reach it so the process of landing fish is made quicker and smoother.

Place your keepnet as close to your feet as possible. You can unhook fish directly over the top and place them in straight afterwards without leaving your seat. To lose a fish when you're match fishing is sacrilege!

IMPROVE YOUR
COARSE
FISHING
THE VIDEO
Waggler Pole and Feeder

ONLY £12.99

Follow **Gareth Purnell** and **John Wilson** as they take you through an hour of waggler tuition, tackling carp...

PLUS

basics of the "lift" method in beautiful lake surroundings, and fishing for barbel on the River Severn.

IMPROVE YOUR COARSE FISHING

THE VIDEO

WAGGLER, POLE AND FEEDER

With John Wilson and editor Gareth Purnell

NOW AVAILABLE FROM ALL

Float Fishing with *Bob Nudd*

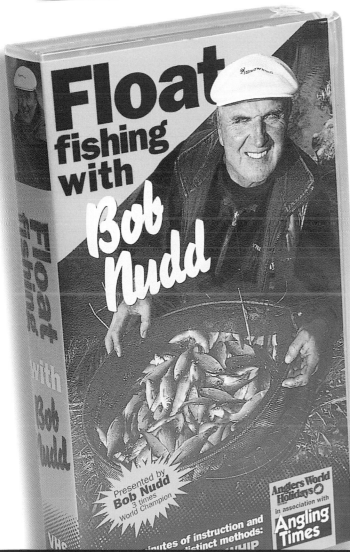

Every second counts!

The more efficient you are at setting up your tackle, the more time you will have catching fish. It may sound obvious, but many anglers get it all wrong. Just follow this advice and make every second count

Humans are creatures of habit. Whether you're changing the oil in your car, cooking a meal, putting your clothes on or shopping, everyone follows a set procedure. Often that procedure is the fastest, simplest and most efficient way to get you where you want to be. It's the same when fishing. Anglers have their own mental step-by-step sequence imprinted in their minds. I'm just the same – every venue I fish is tackled in exactly the same way.

Years of experience

Much time spent on the match circuit has forced me to get organised quickly. After all, when fishing a match you arrive at your peg with around an hour to spare before the whistle blows. In this short time I have to organise my peg, mix my groundbait, sort my bait, set up my pole, then rig-up a whip, waggler or feeder rod as well! The pressure is on, everything has to be perfect and all the time the clock is ticking.

I'm positive the method I, and the majority of match anglers adopt, is one of the most efficient there is. Why not make your fishing that bit more efficient and try it out for yourselves...

After you have set your stall out, ie placed your seat box, baitwaiter, pole roller etc, the next major step is to mix your groundbait if you intend using it. The reason why this should be your first step is because every type of groundbait needs to be left alone for at least five minutes after wetting. This gives enough time for the mix to

◄ *Bob with just one of his flowing water mixes, VDE Super Match and Brown Crumb.*

absorb all the liquid. For the session shown on these pages, on the Great Ouse in the centre of St Neots, Cambridgeshire, I am using a 50/50 (half-and-half) mix of Van Den Eynde's Super Match and Brown Crumb.

I have selected these because together they form a lovely, sticky ball which is ideal for cupping into the swim. Each ball, when you have squeezed it to the correct pressure, sinks straight to the bottom before breaking up. Super Match is a great all-round groundbait which will attract all manner of fish. The crushed hempseed within the mix draws in roach, skimmers and bigger bream, while the dark colouration and smell attracts perch and gudgeon.

Mix it properly

I empty and mix the dry contents into my round bowl. When I'm sure the contents are thoroughly mixed I begin adding water a little at a time to the centre of the groundbait bowl. I quickly spread the water around the mix using my fingers until all the crumb is dampened. To make further stages of the groundbait mixing process easier I rub a little at a time in-between both hands to break up any lumps. Now it's time to leave the groundbait and move over to another subject, making use of every second.

Today the river is running well, the air temperature is cold, as is the water temperature. Experience tells me that I will get bites, but they won't be easy to come by. In simple terms; the water is moving constantly, so the fish in the river need to combat the flow so they are on the move too. They will be using vital energy and therefore require food to replace that energy – that's the reason I know I will get bites. I know they will be hard to come by because it's cold – I will have to work hard.

I suspect the target fish for today's session are roach and hopefully chub – a superb, match winning fish that will feed whatever the weather... I hope!

I opt to fish two lines using two

▲ *Here, Bob's ready to fish the Great Ouse at St Neots. He has plumbed the river depth on both sides (arrows and dotted lines), essential to find dips, snags or other things that may prove to be obstacles to float and hookbait.*

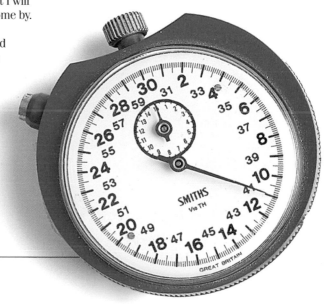

▲ *Spread the water around the mix until all the crumb is nicely dampened.*

▲ *To make mixing easier, rub a little at a time between the fingers, to break up any lumps.*

▲ *Now is the time to match the first rig to the flow of the river. Make a suitable selection.*

floats. Every angler should do this – it gives twice the chance of catching. Now it's time to match my first rig to the flow of the river.

After looking through my many pole rigs I select a body-up version, one which looks like an upturned pear, which is ideal for holding back. It's a Trabucco Camp attached to 13ft of line (shown opposite) and weighted with a 2gr olivette together with a few small 'dropper' shot below.

I know this instantly because each of my winders have labels stuck to their sides, on which line length, line diameter, float weight and shotting pattern is written. This float is for my far, 12m line.

Hook and linelength

Next I select a suitable hook and hooklength. I tie mine at home and store them in a small wallet. A size 22 Browning Maggot attached to 12 inches of 0.08mm Browning Cenitan line (2 lb breaking strain) will do. I tie this, using the loop to loop method, to the end of my rig. Now to find the depth. The groundbait's still waiting and the clock's still ticking.

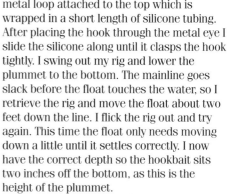

Plumbing not only reveals any changes in the depth, it also tells me exactly how strong the flow is. This I bear in mind for my second, 8m rig.

I always use a brass plummet having a metal loop attached to the top which is wrapped in a short length of silicone tubing. After placing the hook through the metal eye I slide the silicone along until it clasps the hook tightly. I swing out my rig and lower the plummet to the bottom. The mainline goes slack before the float touches the water, so I retrieve the rig and move the float about two feet down the line. I flick the rig out and try again. This time the float only needs moving down a little until it settles correctly. I now have the correct depth so the hookbait sits two inches off the bottom, as this is the height of the plummet.

Plumbing both sides

I plumb to my left and to my right so as to find any dips, snags, or obstacles which may hinder the passage of my float and hookbait. The groundbait is still waiting.

The next stage is to run my rig, without a hookbait, through the swim to see if it snags anywhere. If it does at various places I simply alter the depth until it runs through smoothly.

If it snags at one area only I will just hold the float back just before reaching the spot so my hookbait flutters up and away from the bottom, riding high of the snag. The reason I don't bait the hook is simply because the float may go under because of a fish.

Marking the depth
I now blacken the line just above the float with a permanent pen to mark the depth. After doing this I plumb the depth of my eight metre line, move the float accordingly and mark the depth for that distance too, repeating the same process adopted for my 12m line. The easy to see blackened line will tell me exactly how much to move the float when I change depth. This method does not rub off, provided you don't move the float over the dark area, and neither does it damage the line in any way. Another great method of marking the depth is to lay the float against the pole with the mainline under

◀ Bob uses a brass plummet with a metal loop at the top. This is wrapped in a length of silicone tubing.

▲ Bob has his hooks ready tied to save time.

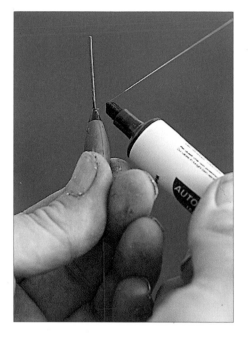

▲ *Blackening the line just above the float.*

▲ *Any lumps are pushed through the riddle.*

tension and simply mark the position on the pole section with a little Tippex.

I turn my attention to my groundbait some ten minutes after first mixing it. About time, I here you cry! The mix has now dried slightly, having absorbed all the water. I now add a little more water and mix it all again with my fingers. After this I riddle it thoroughly, using a specially designed groundbait riddle. These don't cost too much, at around the £12.00 mark, and are well worth the investment. Any larger lumps settling in my riddle are pushed through gently so as not to waste the most nutritious particles. I add a scattering of casters and flouro pinkies and form a ball to

see how it sticks together. A perfect ball should feel spongy, which this now does. It's ready to be used.

Special design

I use a specially-designed top four kit for introducing balls of groundbait. At the very end of my cut-back tip section there is a glued-in screw thread. Onto the end of this I

8m 12m

▲ Bob's home-made cups, designed for introducing balls of groundbait. These cup dispensers are easy as pie to make, yet are extremely serviceable.

◀ The 8 and 12-metre lines are marked on the picture. Four balls of groundbait (shown in the circled picture) are introduced to the 12m line, while three slightly smaller balls are dropped at 8m.

◀ The perfect bait ball – spongy and ready for action!

▶ With his rig ready, Bob's now prepared for some serious pole fishing.

can attach either a small blue cup or a large red cup. Both are home-made, from an aerosol cap, a Brillcream lid and a bolt which is glued to the outside. I form a groundbait ball and place it inside the largest cup, gently ship out and attach my top four kit to the remainder of my pole. Upon reaching 12m I lean out and tip the contents of the cup slightly upstream of my swim. The ball drops

out, hits the water and sinks to the bottom.

Leaning out

The reason for leaning the pole out is because the top four section that I have on at the moment has been cut-back such a long way it's noticeably shorter than my elasticated top four.

I obviously want my bait to pass directly

over the groundbait so leaning out compensates for the loss of pole length. Four balls are introduced to my 12m line and three slightly smaller balls are dropped at 8m.

This whole process has taken a matter of several minutes, but not a second has been wasted. I'm certain that my initial rig, feeding, depth and two swims are ready for action. Now I'm ready to get fishing!

Find those fish

I t's no good trotting a bait through a river swim and just hoping a fish will accept your bait. It takes a lot more thought than that as Bob shows in the next four pages

H aving organised my peg, tackled up, fed both my lines and plumbed the depth accurately, I am finally ready for the most exciting part of the session – catching some fish. Now it's time for probably the most difficult part of the day - finding where the fish are. I have to calculate at what depth they are lying, and whether they will feed or not. Only time and a great deal of hard work will tell. But things are looking good, as another angler, who is fishing upstream of the bridge on my right, tells me this peg is solid with roach. I only hope he's right!

As I've mentioned previously, both my eight and 12m lines have been groundbaited with a few flouro pinkies and a scattering of casters. But, as an extra incentive to persuade any of those passing fish to feed, I will also introduce half a pouchful of red maggots, by catapult, every few minutes. This is my first job before shipping out with a baited hook.

Loosefeeding while holding a pole

Many pole anglers struggle with loosefeeding while holding their pole, but it really is a simple process that is mastered in a matter of minutes.

The major consideration you must bear in mind at all times is to use your catapult in reverse. This may sound a little odd, but it is by far the simplest way to loosefeed while holding a pole.

Follow these simple steps and you too will be able to loosefeed without hassle.

If you have positioned your footplate correctly, so that your thighs are parallel with the horizon as described previously, you will be able to

◄ *Don't forget to lubricate your pole elastic before every session.*

▶ *Loosefeeding while holding a pole is simple when you know how.*

▶ *Loosefeeding while holding a pole is simple when you know how.*

fish with your pole pressed tightly onto the top of your leg with your forearm. You can loosefeed and strike in this position without having to move the pole at all.

The method I have employed for the past 'umpteen' years involves leaving my catapult, with its pouch facing skywards, on the top of my baitwaiter throughout the session. This enables me to fill the pouch and pick up the catapult without taking my eyes off the float. I've done this throughout my angling career, ultimately making the process an almost completely automatic one.

Pointing the catapult

When I have filled the pouch with loosefeed I simply hold the pouch in my right hand (the one that is also pressing down on the pole). Now, instead of pulling the pouch back towards my body, I push the catapult away from my body. Then I point the catapult at my chosen loosefeed area, in this case around eight feet upstream of my groundbaited area, and let the pouch go.

The reason why I choose to loosefeed red maggot so far upstream of my initial groundbait is to combat the strong flow. Having already calculated the depth as being just over 8ft I know my maggots will hit the bottom very close to my groundbait, hopefully turning the heads of any fish nearby making them feed.

You may be asking, why loosefeed big red maggots, instead of flouro pinkies, as that is what you put in your groundbait initially? Well, the answer to this is easy – pinkies, or squatts for that matter, are so lightweight they are swept extremely long distances with the flow before they settle on the bottom. If I was to use those baits I would only end up

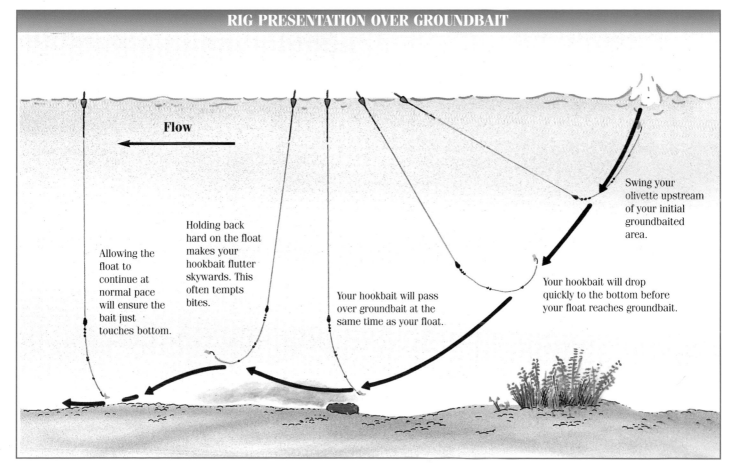

RIG PRESENTATION OVER GROUNDBAIT

Flow ←

Allowing the float to continue at normal pace will ensure the bait just touches bottom.

Holding back hard on the float makes your hookbait flutter skywards. This often tempts bites.

Your hookbait will pass over groundbait at the same time as your float.

Swing your olivette upstream of your initial groundbaited area.

Your hookbait will drop quickly to the bottom before your float reaches groundbait.

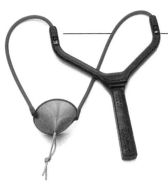

▶ Bob's first fish came an hour into this session.

If I were to select a yellow or black tipped float I would never have spotted the bite as the reflections on the water surface are both black and white. In these conditions the best float tip colour is red as it stands out against both background colours. If the water was completely black I would use a yellow tipped float, if it is dazzling white, I would use a black tipped float. It's common sense really.

My first bite produces a small roach for the net and a confidence boost for me. This is because roach are not dissimilar to bream in being a shoaling fish - so where there's one, there will hopefully be others. And when one fish feeds others follow.

Biting fish and bait

The bite came when I was running the float through my swim at around half the river's pace - perhaps that is how the fish want the bait today. This can often be the case at any time of year - one day the fish will happily accept a static bait, the next day they will

splitting up whatever shoal is already in my swim, or, the fish may be held a long way down my peg - well out of pole reach.

Red maggot results

Ideally, the best loosefeed I could introduce here today would be hemp as it drops through the depths so quickly, but I do not intend using it as I'm sure I would achieve better results with red maggot - so here I go.

Before fishing with a pole I always lubricate my elastic. There are two reasons why I do this. First, it allows a free passage of elastic through the bush, and secondly the lubricant displaces any dirt which has entered the pole tip. I always use a bottled lubricant from Preston Innovations, but there are many different versions available nowadays.

I hook a single, large juicy maggot and ship out until I reach my groundbaited 12m line, then gently swing the pole two or three metres to my right so the olivette and hookbait hits the water upstream of my float. I have picked this method up over the years and it is perfect when fishing an olivette, or bulk shot rig, over the top of groundbait. You can see why in the diagram on the previous page. When the olivette hits the water it drops, not in a straight line to the bottom, but in an arc. My float stays almost static. It will move downstream, but only a fraction.

I allow the float to sail along with the current until it reaches my groundbaited area. Now, the olivette and dropper shot have settled and my hookbait is dragging, at the speed of the current, through the scented cloud formed by my 50/50 mix of Van Den

Eynde Super Match and brown crumb. If there are any fish rooting through the groundbait at that time there's no way they would be able to resist my hookbait offering.

As is often the case when fishing another tactic is called for, and it is to make the bait a little more attractive. I make this happen by holding the float back as soon as it is positioned over the groundbait.

I used a static far bank marker when I cupped my initial groundbait into the swim, so when the float is level with that, a telegraph pole, I tighten the line between pole tip and float, ultimately stopping the float dead in its tracks. This doesn't stop my hookbait though. The maggot tantalisingly flutters upwards, through the scented groundbait cloud. This often induces bites, but if they aren't forthcoming I slacken line between pole tip and float so my hookbait drifts along with the flow once more.

Searching for best results

Fishing a river with a pole in this way is very similar to stick float fishing. All the time I'm making changes to the rig and the speed at which it passes through the swim. The fish may be hard on the bottom, or they may be a couple of feet off the bottom - so I must search all these areas throughout the session to gain the best results.

After an hour of fruitless searching both lines, eight and 12m, and continual loosefeeding I am rewarded with my first bite. My float's fluorescent orange tip vanishes from sight directly above my groundbait. Things are looking up at last!

only look twice at a bait that is hurtling towards them at the full pace of the river.

Both the aforementioned techniques are relatively simple to master when pole fishing. Holding back requires the angler to keep the pole tip steady in order to halt the bait. Running a bait through the swim is just a case of moving the pole tip around with the river's flow.

Unfortunately, running a baited hook through a swim at half pace is a little more difficult. First of all you have to maintain a tight line between pole tip and float, but not too tight so as the float rides right out of the water and halts the bait. What's more you have to have total control of your pole - again, pressing the butt section onto your thigh using your forearm is by far the best method. Never, under any circumstances sit on your pole. Not only have you a higher chance of

◄ *Always use a good brand of lubricant for your pole elastic.*

breaking it, you are not in direct contact when a fish bites.

One excellent method I use to help make trotting a float at half-pace easier is to add a little more shot to the rig. In this instance I am adding another No8 shot, which will sink the rig instantly. Now, when fishing, I literally have to hold the float up with my mainline or else it will sink registering false bites.

This method takes a little practise, but once mastered provides you with a perfect trot through the swim.

This method can also be employed when the fish require a bait which is held back hard, or totally static. To do this simply add a little more shot, then you have to have an almost vertical line between pole tip and float to ensure the tip is protruding from the water.

Three average sized roach and the first chub of the session fall to this deadly method within a matter of minutes.

The next time you're pole fishing your local river give it a try – what are you waiting for?

▼ *When fishing a bulk shot or olivette rig over a bed of groundbait, it is imperative that you swing the weight upstream of the float, before trotting the swim.*

Don't just sit there!

If you were to choose the right pattern hook to match your bait, or the correct mainline for your pole elastic, would you get it right every time? Read on, and you'll be doing it as well as the triple world champ...

My constant bombardment of maggot loosefeed has finally persuaded the Great Ouse roach to feed in confidence. Every other trot through at half the pace of the river, which flows through St Neots, in Cambridgeshire, is producing either a bite or a fish. It really is great fishing. It really has taken a lot of effort to get my swims going this time, but the hard work is starting to pay off.

This is typical of how I match fish, always changing tactics in order to gain as many bites and fish as quickly as possible in the hope of winning either the match or my section. Although this description fits that of a typical match angler, it should also be true for pleasure anglers, too. Changes have to be made to bait, rigs, feeding and tactics to maintain a constant run of bites, or the fish will quickly lose interest. It's no good just placing your rod in a rest and sitting back enjoying the sun's rays. You won't learn anything adopting this method, unless you are specimen carp angler fishing with boilies.

Getting the best

To get the best from any swim, be it on a river, canal or stillwater, you must remember to feed two or more lines. This gives you an option which is very important indeed because if one of your feeding areas suddenly becomes fishless, you can always move over to your second line of attack. It's really simple, all you need do is locate two or more features, such as a ledge, a mass of weeds or a deep hole and groundbait one or both. Then simply loosefeed maggot, caster, hemp etc over

▲ *To make things go well, set your rig length so that small fish can be swung directly into your hand without fuss.*

the top. I guarantee that if you adopt this method you will catch more fish and become a better angler by doing so.

Struggling for bites

Bites on my 12m line have started to slow down a little, and I'm beginning to struggle for bites. I have been trying my 8m line at intervals throughout the session, but bites were not forthcoming. I do believe fish are still around my furthest line, but they have moved somewhere and I must find them again.

The pole that I am using, the Browning B7500, is capable of reaching 14.5m, so this enables me to search a wider area, but first of all it is worth trying a little closer, at 11m. This doesn't produce bites, so the fish must be either further out in the central flow or sitting well away from the groundbait. Another reason why a swim can suddenly go quiet is the arrival of a pike, a fish that always manages to spook a shoal.

Adding another two sections to my pole allows me to search beyond my 12m line and it also allows me to trot my float a little further downstream. This works a treat! On the second trot through, a fish takes the bait and a 4oz roach is in the net.

I've found the fish again and they are a little downstream and a little further out than my initial groundbaited area. If I can tempt them back to my groundbait, at 12m, I will stand a much better chance of hitting every bite, simply because it is a little easier to control a pole at this length rather than at 14.5m.

▼ *Bob's pole for this session is a real whopper, the Browning 7500.*

BROWNING. TITANIUM B7500

Into the keepnet

I actually swung the last fish to hand. This is by far the easiest and fastest way to get a hooked fish into your keepnet, providing the fish you hook is small enough to do so. Experience will tell you what size fish are suitable to be swung-in, and you must have faith in your terminal tackle, or disasters will occur. Never, under any circumstances, swing large fish to hand, or small fish when you are using very light hooklengths, say 0.06 or 0.07mm.

All you do is play the fish as normal and unship the pole as you go. Always remember

▲ *Feeding two or more lines gets the best from any swim, whether it is a river, stillwater or a canal. Remember to keeping changing tactics, as this is what gets the bites.*

▲ This hungry 10oz chub was absolutely full of Bob's loosefed red maggots.

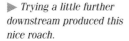 ▶ Trying a little further downstream produced this nice roach.

to break the pole down at the appropriate point, for example, if your rig is 3.5m long, break the pole at the fourth section. The weight of the fish will pull a little elastic from the tip of your pole, therefore extending your rig length. Then you can gently lift the pole sections skywards, until the fish emerges from the water. Continue moving the pole upwards, lifting the fish out as you go. Try to ensure the fish is swung into your chest and grab it gently with your free hand as it approaches.

Unhooking the fish

Now that you have a pole in one hand and a fish in the other, how do you unhook the fish? I just push the pole section I am holding under my arm, press it into my side to clasp the pole section tight. This leaves a hand free to unhook the fish.

I always keep my disgorger tied around my neck with a little string. I don't use elastic as the disgorger may get stuck in my zip or something and twang back into my eye! Having your disgorger on a string is extremely handy as you always know where it is. There's no more fumbling around when you have to unhook. I now prefer to use Stonfo's new double-headed version which is actually three tools in one. At one end there is a large disgorger which is ideal for use with larger hooks, say sizes 16 and above.

The other end features a smaller disgorger for the remaining hook sizes. In the middle there is also a sharp, steel knot picker. This is a godsend when you are faced with a tangle. The next couple of attempts with maggot are not successful, so it's time to try casters instead. Whenever I have completed a trot or two through the swim I check my bait for

signs of damage. Fish don't always drag the float under when they bite, so a quick check on the bait ensures it hasn't been tampered with in any way. This method obviously involves swinging the bait to hand, but there is another way to check on a bait which will speed up the process. This is best employed when fishing either caster or bread on the hook, as these two baits are often either pulled directly off the hook, or chewed by fish. All you do is lift the rig from the water and raise the pole tip until you can see either the hook or bait silhouetted against the sky. Now you can spot whether the bait has fallen off the hook, has been chewed, or is intact.

Using the pole

Whatever venue you are fishing, be it a stillwater, river or canal, you must use the pole as an extension to your own arm, as you

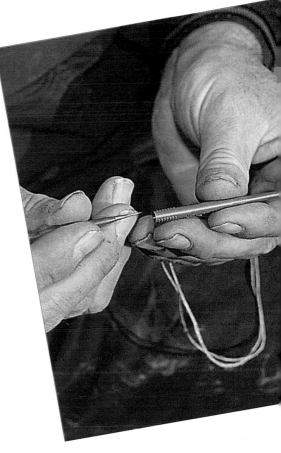

◀ The St Neots session has been quite hard work, and that's what makes this mixed bag of fish such a rewarding way to end the day.

would with a rod. In time you will feel at ease pole fishing, and every movement will eventually become second nature. Absolutely anyone can easily get to grips with this often deadly method. Even if you are not the tidiest of float anglers, when you use a pole your presentation will be bettered almost immediately.

Limitations of pole fishing

You can push your terminal tackle close to weeds, lilies or snags, and if you get a bite and miss it, you need not waste time by winding in your rig and recasting. Pole fishing does have its limitations. Obviously you can only fish the same distance as your pole, give or take a few metres, and you definitely cannot use poles when fishing for specimen sized carp, barbel or catfish as they will easily break either your line, elastic or worse

still, your pole. Anyway, back to the session.

Bites were not forthcoming using caster as hookbait, so I've changed back to red maggot, and the second trot through produces the first chub of the day, albeit quite small, at around eight ounces. This is extremely promising, as looking down the chub's throat as I unhooked it reveals it to be full of pinkies and red maggots. Obviously the fish had settled onto my groundbait, munching both the loosefed maggots and groundbaited pinkies as he did so. Great news! This may mean there are more small chub there for the taking or the odd larger fish as a bonus. This bite came when I held the float back hard directly over my groundbait, as previously described, so I intend continuing this method for a few trots through the swim to see if it produces any more weight building chub – and it does.

Soon after my number two elastic stretches from the pole tip under the pressure of the largest chub of the day, a fine, fin perfect 1lb 6oz fish. My pole, having a 'tip action only' absorbs the fight beautifully, and the fish is soon beaten, brought to the surface and drawn over the net. Great!

I am now five hours into the session and the light is beginning to fade. Bites still aren't coming thick and fast, so I think it is about time I called it a day. As with all anglers, I'd much rather stay here on the banks of the River Ouse and catch a few more fish. I have taken a very nice net of roach and small chub, plus a larger chub as a bonus.

I've thoroughly enjoyed my session here at St Neots and more to the point, I've thoroughly enjoyed explaining all the ins and outs of polefishing a river during the last few pages. I hope you have enjoyed it too.

World-class angling

Here we take a quick break from the nitty-gritty details of pole angling, and take a look at some of Bob's match-winning events of the last few years

Bob Nudd is rightly regarded around the world as one of the top match anglers of all time, having proved himself time and time again at the very highest levels of competition. As you might imagine, his record for England in the world championships is second to none. Since being included in the squad for the first time back in 1984, this regular contributor to *Improve* *Your Coarse Fishing* magazine has missed only one match, in 1987, and then he was in the squad.

The first medal

Bob's first medal, a team silver, came in his very first world championships in Switzerland, and his first team gold the following year while competing on the River Arno in Italy. He took the first of his many World Championship section wins in 1988 in Belgium, helping the team to another gold medal. But it was two years later that Bob's amazing run of individual success began.

Continued page 50 ▶

▼*A happy England team line up for their victory photograph in Belgium*

▶ It's dateline 1991, as Bob shows off his match-winning catch after victory in Hungary.

◀ This is what match angling is all about – gold and silver medals hanging proudly by their multi-coloured neckbands.

It was in 1990, on Yugoslavia's deep and fast-flowing River Drava, that Bob took two section wins, thus easily pocketing the individual gold and winning another team medal, this time a silver. Bob then went on to really amaze the angling world by retaining his individual crown in 1991 in Hungary with another two section wins. With this victory he became the first angler ever to achieve the feat. For England it was another superb triumph, with the England squad again taking the team gold.

Bob's greatest triumph?

But perhaps Bob's greatest triumph of all came back on home turf in 1994, when he won a third individual gold on Nottingham's rock-hard Holme Pierrepont rowing course. This was a victory gained in front of a packed crowd of thousands of adoring home fans. England again took the team gold in that match under the leadership of Dick Clegg. By early 1998, Bob had managed to total a big-time tally of medals – three individual golds, five team golds, four team silvers and a team bronze. Truly a world class angler!

▲ The England team line up for the 1994 Holme Pierrepont awards. Here Bob scored in both Team and Individual golds.

▲ It's Holme Pierrepont 1994, and Bob gets mobbed by scores of wellwishers.

▶ Bob shows off his catch at Holme Pierrepont 1994, with extra congratulations from his wife, Bernadette.

▲ An enthusiastic crowd packs in behind the protection barriers as Bob fishes his way to outright victory at Holme Pierrepont, 1991.

▶ It's a visit to the victory podium once again for the England team. This time the prize the anglers have taken is the Team silver, won against hard competition on the River Mincio in Italy, 1996.

Everything to play for

Tackling carp on the pole requires balanced tackle, strong equipment, continual loosefeeding and above all, nerves of steel. In the next pages Bob gives an in-depth account of what is required to catch your first netful of carp

If you have ever hooked and played a carp while using a pole you will appreciate the sheer enjoyment it brings. Your elastic bottoms out, the fish drags your pole all over the lake and your mainline zig-zags through the water surface, whistling under the immense strain. As you can tell, your pole, line and tackle are tested to the limit. Every item must be balanced, or disaster will strike.

But there are ways of preventing disaster, particularly if you are solely targeting carp. In these pages I intend running you through what is required to get those hard fighting cyprinids to the net, the correct tackle you require, some invaluable tactics for playing the fish and information on some For this carp session I have chosen to fish Brookhall lake, near Tiptree, Essex. It is heavily stocked with carp, mainly mirrors averaging 3lb, with the addition of roach and bream.

Fishing can be excellent here, but you do have to work very hard to keep a steady flow of fish coming to the net. However, this is the case on every venue and for every species, as you will see later. The record five hour match weight here is a whopping 195lb – great fishing in anyone's book, especially during match conditions.

I have done a little research on the venue to find out how it has been fishing, and what

baits and tactics are working. I have found that the fish are taking trout pellets, paste, sweetcorn and luncheon meat in open water and also tight to marginal weed.

Effort and tactics

Every angler should put in the same effort wherever he or she is going. This saves a great deal of time and effort when you are fishing, but you must always have the flexibility to change tactics if you are not catching. As is often the case, fish can change their routine overnight. For example, on Tuesday the fish may have been feeding confidently in mid-water taking the bait on-the-drop, but on Wednesday, the day you are fishing, there may have been a heavy frost overnight and the fish will be hugging the bottom, where the water is warmest. There is a moral to this, and it is that you must be prepared to alter tactics to tempt the fish.

I have decided to fish peg 15, here at Brookhall. It is almost in the centre of this coloured, rectangular lake. There is a little

fish-holding weed in the margins to both my right and left and open water directly in front of me.

I intend fishing three lines using three rigs and four tactics. Sounds a little confusing, but it is simple really!

My first line is four metres to my left, and about four feet from the bank, tight to nearside vegetation. The second is the same distance out, but to my right. My third and fourth lines are both at 10 metres, but one is hard on the bottom, the other will be up in the water. All I need to do know is to select the correct style of rig to suit all my four lines.

In my research on the venue I found the best baits to be either trout pellets, sweetcorn, paste or luncheon meat. Baits like maggots, casters etc are not taking fish at the moment. This means the unconventional baits I have to use are extremely heavy in comparison to maggots or casters. This ultimately means that I have to alter my float designs to suit the extra weight of the bait. If I

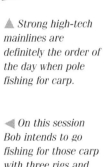

▲ *Strong high-tech mainlines are definitely the order of the day when pole fishing for carp.*

◀ *On this session Bob intends to go fishing for those carp with three rigs and four tactics.*

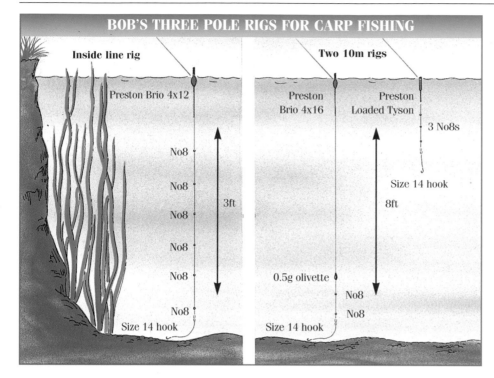

BOB'S THREE POLE RIGS FOR CARP FISHING

Inside line rig

Preston Brio 4x12

No8

No8

No8

No8

No8

3ft

No8

Size 14 hook

Two 10m rigs

Preston Brio 4x16

Preston Loaded Tyson

3 No8s

Size 14 hook

8ft

0.5g olivette

No8

No8

Size 14 hook

▲ *Bob forms an 18-inch loop in the end of his elastic, to act as a buffer when playing carp.*

▲ *Don't forget to lubricate your elastic.*

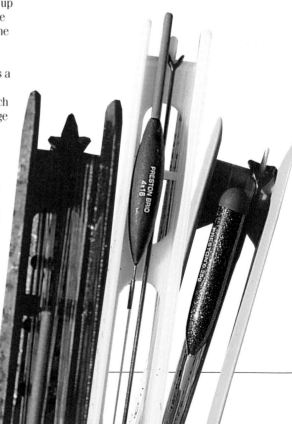

was to use a standard, slender fibre glass bristled float the bait would pull the tip under every single time, especially when attempting to fish a bait at mid-water. So with this in mind I have deliberately chosen three floats, all of which have extremely buoyant bristles.

Extra-strong line

The first, which I intend using for both my right and left hand marginal lines, is set upon a 4x12 Preston Innovations' Brio float having a thick buoyant bristle. The mainline for this rig is 0.15mm (4.5lb breaking strain) and the hooklength is 0.13mm (3.5lb), both being Cenitan XC high-tech line. This is an extra-strong line that will allow me to bully fish away from the nearby weed if they bolt towards it at any stage.

The shotting pattern is quite simple; six number eight shot set shirt button style down the mainline. This gives a slow fall of the hookbait and also plenty of time for nearby fish to spot the bait as it drops. The hook attached to the eight inch hooklength is a strong size 14 Browning Chikara Barbless Specimen.

After looking through my many spare pole top kits I've selected a telescopic top three which has number 12 elastic running through all three sections. This extra strong elastic allows me to bully the fish away from the near bank weeds.

For my far line, at 10 metres, I have picked two rigs. The first, for presenting a bait on the bottom, is again, a Preston Innovations' Brio requiring 4x16 styles to cock it correctly. Instead of having a string of number eight squeezed onto the mainline, I have attached a

small 0.5g olivette set two feet from the hook, followed by two number eight shot as droppers. These are set upon 0.13mm (3.5lb breaking strain) mainline, with eight inches of 0.12mm (3lb) hooklength attached to it. Again, the hook is a large, strong size 14 Barbless Specimen. This is presented under three sections of number eight elastic. I haven't used too strong an elastic for this rig as the bites will be gentle and there aren't any snags in the middle of the lake, so there is no need to bully the fish anyway. If there were lilies or weeds in the middle I would step up two or three strengths in order to stop the fish in their tracks, before they reached the snags.

The rig I intend using to present a bait between two and three feet deep features a Preston Innovations' Loaded Tyson float. This is a reinforced dibber style float which will be able to cope with the fight of a large carp. Its dome-shaped tip forms part of the balsa body and is therefore very buoyant indeed.

Preparing for powerful bites

The mainline is 0.13mm (3.5lb) and the hooklength is 0.12mm (3lb). The shotting consists of three number eights spread evenly down the line and to finish off I have tied on the same strong size 14 hook. Because the bites are often powerful when fishing up in the water for carp I have attached this rig to a telescopic top three containing eight feet of number ten elastic.

I am using my trusty Browning Nickel Reflex pole for today's session.

▲ *Note how far Bob has cut his tip section in order to accommodate the thicker elastics.*

It is extremely strong and more than capable of playing any match-sized carp. On all three of my top kits I have cut back the tip section quite a fair way, in order that the thick elastics can pass through the tip smoothly and easily.

On the subject of elastics, I have 'doubled-up' mine at the bung. By this I mean I have passed my elastic through the bung and formed a long, 18 inch loop. This is imperative when carp fishing because, when the fish bottoms the single length of elastic out it still has to fight against a doubled length. So if I am using a number ten elastic and the fish stretches it to its limit, the loop will begin to stretch, and that is equivalent to number 20 elastic. There is no way a carp will be able to bottom that length out!

Plumbing the depths

The next stage is to plumb the depth of the three areas I intend fishing. I attach my plummet to the hook, ship my rig out to the desired area and allow the rig to fall through the water until the plummet gently touches the bottom. If my float goes under I know it is set too shallow, if it stands proud of the water it is set too deep.

I have found that both my nearside swims to be three feet deep so I have pushed my float up the line a little so that the bait lays on

▲ *Bob went for top three kits containing strong No8, 10 and 12 elastics.*

the bottom three inches over depth.

My ten-metre swim turned out to be eight feet deep and again I moved the float up the line so I am presenting my bait four inches overdepth. I needn't plumb the depth of my swim up in the water rig as that would be stupid! I simply guess the depth at which the fish will be feeding and simply go from there to see how it works.

Ready to start

My rigs are now ready for action – all that is left is to tidy my peg, make some final amendments to my tackle and sort my bait. Everything's prepared – all my sundry tackle items are close at hand and my spare three top kits are positioned off the ground to prevent damage. My bait waiter is set upon a bankstick and positioned to my left. I have my pole roller set at the correct distance from my body, so as the pole balances well when shipping out. The keepnet is down by my feet and my landing net is ready and waiting for those fish.

As always, I have squirted a fair amount of lubricant into my top three sections so the elastic slips from the pole tip as smoothly and efficiently as possible.

All I need to do now is sort out my bait for the session and feed the three swims. I simply can't wait to get started...

Liquid gold

If Bob is sitting in front of a frantically feeding shoal of carp he's a happy man. But it takes constant loosefeeding to get a shoal of carp competing for his bait

One of the most crucial aspects of carp fishing is the feeding. Once you have the fish feeding on your loosefeed, fighting for every single morsel, sport can be absolutely incredible. But turning your swim into a bubbling cauldron of hungry carp can be a lengthy process which requires plenty of care and thought.

I have my tackle ready, my peg is clear and comfortable. All that is left is to begin the feeding process.

For this session, I intend to go fishing with three lines, using four rigs. The first two lines are right next to nearside weed four metres to my left and four metres to my right. This is almost always a hot patrolling route for carp

as they usually tend to follow the contours of the lake, along the nearside ledge, hunting for food. Here I will cup in a fair amount of loosefeed, and introduce bait over the top at regular intervals. Both my third and fourth lines are directly in front of me, 10 metres out. The first rig for this area is set slightly overdepth, the second is a buoyant dibber rig for fishing up-in-the-water.

In cold water

Although the temperature during the night dropped drastically and the water is fairly cold this morning, I know I will tempt the carp off the bottom at some point during the session. This is exactly what I am

aiming for, as I can catch more carp with my bait set at mid-depth than I can with the bait on the bottom. Let me explain why...

First of all I need to get the fish into my swim. To do this I will cup in some loosefeed offerings right at the start. Eventually fish will find this bait an begin to eat it. At this early stage I will fish with my bait on the bottom, seeking the odd fish which moves into my swim.

All the time I will loosefeed over the top. I won't put in too much loosefeed at the start as the water is cold, so the fish don't need much food, and there won't be enough fish in my swim to eat it all.

I have three pints of trout pellets purely for

loosefeeding. They are a superb bait for loosefeeding, particularly with a catapult, as they make a lovely sound as they enter the water. This sound really attracts fish into your swim – they smell the trout pellets and stay there, waiting for more pellets to land on their heads.

Snatching at the bait

As more and more carp move into the swim they will begin to compete for the constant stream of pellets falling through the water. They will rush for every morsel, darting through the water in an attempt to get the most food. Every time a pouchful of trout pellets hits the water the fish will respond by swimming upwards, snatching at the baits as they fall. The fish which gets the most bait is the one which is highest in the shoal, and that is the time that you should switch rigs and fish your bait up-in-the-water. So let's now start cupping some feed in and begin fishing.

My initial loosefeeding bait is exactly the same for all three lines – half a cupful of soaked trout pellets, topped off by some tiny cubes of luncheon meat.

I would normally prepare my luncheon meat at home if I were fishing a match, but

▲ *Remember that you need to have your hookpoint showing, even if it is only a fraction of a centimetre.*

◄ *Bob maintains a constant loosefeeding pattern, firing trout pellets into his swim every few minutes. Nice 'n' Spicy luncheon meat proves a deadly delight for greedy carp.*

for today's purposes I'll prepare it on the bank to show you how it's done.

I have also added some water to my trout pellets to soften them a little. Although they are sinking pellets, when you cup them into your swim they often just float off, because they have fallen so gently they haven't broken the surface tension of the water.

I have also added a big squirt of Van Den

▼ *Bob loosefeeds each swim with half a cupful of trout pellets, topped with luncheon meat.*

▲ *Bob cuts a full section of meat into three strips, using a sharp knife.*

▲ *One by one, he pushes each strip of meat through a maggot riddle.*

▲ *The finished product – finely chopped meat that makes perfect loosefeed.*

Eynde's Liquid Pellet. This is an extremely good feed inducer. It is actually the same oily, fishy additive which is sprayed onto trout pellets to make them more attractive to fish.

When the pellets soften adequately I also have another option of using them on the hook, but at the moment they are too hard to get a hook through them. They will take about an hour to soften.

Meat for loosefeeding

The meat I am using isn't ordinary shop-bought luncheon meat – it is Van Den Eynde's Nice 'n' Spicy meat. It is superb year-round bait for carp, but especially good when the water is cold. Fish respond better to spicy flavoured baits during colder weather. In high summer Van Den Eynde's sweet-smelling strawberry meat will work better.

Preparing the meat for loosefeeding couldn't be simpler. After opening a tin, I slice the full tubular piece of meat into four sections, each being 1.5cm thick. Then I place the meat onto my round maggot riddle and push the slices, one by one, through the riddle.

This transforms the slices into tiny cubes, all being small enough not to fill the fish up. They also have a large surface area in proportion to the size which allows plenty of the meat's lovely, spicy smell to dissolve into the water, ultimately attracting fish towards your hookbait. Their large surface area to size also makes the meat fall through the water very slowly indeed, so any passing fish will have plenty of time to spot the falling baits and home in on them.

I have introduced one cupful on both my four metre, inside lines, and three large cupfuls on my far, 10-metre line. To help remember exactly where I cupped in on my 10-metre line I lined my pole tip with a far-bank marker – in this case a post.

Main line of attack

I will leave both my inside lines to 'brew' for a while. I won't forget about them though, as they still require a constant stream of loosefeed. Carp often need quite a while to become confident enough to feed close to the margins and close to bankside disturbance, so my main line of attack will be at ten metres.

My first rig of this session is set around a Preston Innovations' Brio 4x16 float set eight feet deep and three inches overdepth. I have attached a slither of luncheon meat onto the large, size 14 hook ready to ship out.

This is a tip well worth noting, and it has

been said a thousand times before, but it is so important if you want to catch fish: Always make sure your hook point is showing. If it isn't you will still get bites, but you won't connect with half of them. If you look carefully at the photograph on the previous page you can just about see the point protruding from the meat. There isn't much of the point showing, but it is enough to get a good hold of the fish.

Now it's about time I shipped out and laid the rig on the surface. I have pushed the float out to the full 10 metres, and now I like to lift up the pole so the hookbait rides out of the water and gently sweep the pole across the water so the rig lies in a straight line, avoiding tangles as I do so. Then I pull the float across the surface until it lies directly between myself and the far-bank marker, a post. When the shot settles and the float sits correctly I know my hookbait is directly over the top of my loosefeed - if it hasn't all been eaten yet! The bait's been in the water for a couple of

◀ *Bob adds a generous squirt of Liquid Pellet to his bait.*

minutes and it's time to loosefeed. I only loosefeed a little at a time, but on a regular basis when fishing for carp, or any other species.

My catapult is always ready, laying on my baitwaiter. I can easily place a few pellets inside the catapult's cup without taking my eyes off the float, and therefore I don't miss any all important bites.

I introduce around ten pellets for every pouchful of loosefeed. They hit the water with a machine gun sound, splattering droplets of water as they hit the surface. Any carp near my swim will pick up the sound, and move in on my loosefeed – hopefully!

Five minutes have passed and no bite. I have loosefed my 10-metre line three times and both my inside lines once. This gives you an idea of how often you need to keep firing in bait.

To check whether the bait is still on the hook I simply raise the pole's tip until the bait pops out of the water. It is still intact so I shall lay the rig out on the surface again.

Moulding pellet paste

There are still no bites, so it's time to change bait. I have also brought with me some ready made paste. There are many pastes available now, both shop bought and home-made versions, but today I am field testing the new Van Den Eynde Pellet Paste. It is lovely and soft, and smells good too!

I pinch off a little paste and mould it around my hook, remembering to keep the hookpoint showing.

Out goes the rig, together with three pouchful of pellets and still no bites, even after five minutes. So it's back to a slither of meat; this time I'll soak it in Liquid Pellet.

The great thing about this additive is its high oil content. You can see a slick of smelly oil forming over my swim everytime I catapult my soaked pellets. There's no way a carp can resist.

In goes the rig and straight away my float nudges from left to right. I don't strike as that was a line bite. There are finally fish in my swim, and it's only taken 15 minutes.

To make my bait a little more appealing I've lifted the pole tip so the bait gently wafts off the bottom and the float darts under straight away.

A sharp strike sets the hook into the first fish of the session. My elastic screeches from the pole and my tip bends round under the pressure. And we're off. It's the Liquid Pellet that has done the trick. Those carp simply can't resist the thick, oily scent it gives off. Now it's time to bag up!

▲ *Bob's soaked trout pellets sink when gently cupped into the water.*

▼ *At last! After some while, and a lot of effort and patience, the first fish of the session finally makes it to the net.*

Fast and furious

When there is a shoal of carp in your swim, all competing for the same loosefeed, action can be frantic, as Bob shows on these pages

My loosefeeding has worked a treat. I have only been fishing peg 15 on Brookhall Lake for a quarter-hour, and I've already hooked into a carp. It's certainly not a giant, by any means, but it is giving a fine account of itself, pulling plenty of elastic from my pole tip. The fish took my bait, a small slither of Van Den Eynde's Nice 'n' Spicy luncheon meat, just before it settled on the bottom. Once the rig settled and the bait reached the bottom, I waited for a couple of minutes. Bites were not immediately forthcoming so I lifted my pole until the Preston Innovations' Brio float rose from the water. This made my bait rise and fall very slowly, a carp saw it and couldn't resist. One-nil to me!

Over the last few minutes I had noticed my float knocking from side to side. I didn't strike at these movements purely because they were line bites. This, to me, indicated there was at least one fish in my swim, possibly two or three. I will find out how many on the next put-in.

I have battled with this small carp for three minutes now and it is beginning to tire. Once I have got the fish to the surface and it takes in a gulp of air it is as good as mine. I've reached for my landing net and placed the net underneath the water. I haven't had to reach far, or get off my box for the net, as it is always right alongside my box, ready for use at any moment.

The carp breaks the surface, giving me an ideal opportunity to gradually 'skim' it along the water's surface, towards my waiting landing net. It goes in perfectly.

Unhooking carp can be a difficult process, especially if you use barbed hooks. Most small carp fisheries have banned the use of barbed hooks simply because carp fight extremely well, often so well they smash the hooklength, even the mainline. If this happens when using barbed hooks, the fish

◀ Catching carp of this size while pole fishing is great fun!

Bob always keeps spare pole sections set up behind to help control larger fish. It's a preparation habit that every pole fishing enthusiast should take to heart, as being prepared like this can make all the difference between a missed opportunity and a good catch.

will have the hook buried inside its mouth for the rest of its days. If the hook is barbless it will eventually fall from the fish's mouth, causing no serious damage. I have tied on barbless hooks on all three of my rigs, as the lake owner, Peter Clapperton, insists on all anglers using them here.

Four-step unhooking

I always follow a simple four-step process when unhooking large fish, such as carp. First of all I lift the fish from the water via my landing net. Then I place the landing net head between my knees so the fish does not touch the ground. Then I unhook the fish using my disgorger which is always tied around my neck. The final step is to transfer the carp from my landing net into my keepnet. This is vitally important as it prevents the fish from either falling back into the water or onto dry ground which may cause all manner of internal damage. Who says match anglers don't care about fish? I certainly do!

I haven't fed my 10-metre line for almost four minutes now, so it's time to catapult another 12 or so trout pellets into my swim.

My hook is baited with another slither of luncheon meat, again soaked in Van Den Eynde's Liquid Pellet, and shipped out into my swim.

After just ten seconds the float cocks and my bait reaches the bottom. Again, the float shudders as a carp bumps into my 0.13mm mainline. A split second later it slides under as a fish takes the bait.

I strike into carp with a very forceful

▲ *To prevent hooked fish swimming back into the shoal, Bob applies as much pressure as his elastic will allow.*

▼ *Bob softens his paste with a little Liquid Pellet to make it more attractive to the fish.*

upward movement of the pole. This sets the hook into the carp's tough lips ensuring a good hold. As with most carp, the fish screams away. Fast reactions and quick evasive action is required to prevent your line or pole breaking.

The carp shoots away from me and to my left, taking plenty of my number eight elastic. When carp run like this you need to be prepared. I have two extra sections of pole set-up behind me to cope with situations like this. All the time the carp is gradually slowing down, but not by a great degree. The only way to stop it is to put on my two spare sections of pole and pull the fish as hard as my elastic will allow.

It works. The carp begins to slow down and turn its head. The elastic is almost at full stretch, so any sharp runs by the fish have to be compensated by releasing a

little pressure on the elastic. To do this I follow the fish around with the pole. If the fish suddenly darts off to the left I will allow the pole to move to the left also, and vice versa.

Breaking down the pole

After a few quick runs the fish begins to tire, giving me an ideal chance to ship the pole back on its roller. Although my rig is only three sections long, I need to break the pole down at the fifth section. This is simply because the heavy carp will have pulled elastic from the pole, technically making my rig at least four-and-a-half sections long from the tip of my pole.

The fish is getting closer all the time, at around eight metres from the bank. Now its time to pile on the pressure using only five sections. I do this by sharply raising the pole tip to get as much elastic out of the pole as I can. This prevents the hooked fish reaching my loosefeed area and possibly spooking the rest of the shoal.

The tired fish is soon in the net, my swim is

fed once more with a few pellets and my baited hook is back in the swim. I have also flicked more pellets over both my inside lines as well.

You will notice that I am not feeding my inside lines as heavily as my far line, perhaps on a ratio of ten to one. This is because I want the fish to come up in the water on my 10-metre line, I don't want this to happen on my inside lines.

Trying another bait

Out goes the rig once more with the same soaked meat bait. This time, although I am still getting line bites, fish will not pick up my bait. After three minutes and two feeds later I retrieve the rig. It's time to try another bait.

I have also brought some Van Den Eynde Pellet Paste to try out. It has the same distinct smell as trout pellets, but it is lovely and soft – you can use it straight from the jar. Hopefully, the fish will accept this bait readily.

To make my paste even softer and more attractive I have mixed in a good squirt of Liquid Pellet. The fish should find this combination extremely hard to resist, making it an extremely good bait. The extra softness also ensures the hook pulls straight through the paste on the strike, but this does cause a few problems.

The paste is now so soft is it quite difficult to ship out into your swim. You certainly couldn't use it on a waggler – it would just fly off the hook upon the cast. So the only way to get this ultra-soft paste into my swim is to ship out carefully and gently.

Out goes the paste, the rig settles, the float bounces around with line bites, but doesn't register a bite. I think it must be time to change tactics.

I have retrieved the rig and fed the line with more pellets. This time swirls appear on the surface immediately after the bait hits the water. It is definitely time to change tactics, the fish are so far up-in-the-water they are almost climbing out!

My rig for fishing with a bait suspended is already set up to my left. All I need to do is bait the hook and ship out. Not a second is wasted. It is amazing that the fish are already high in the water. There was a slight frost last night, which would have forced the fish to the bottom, but within only an hour of fishing they have moved up to intercept the passing loosefeed offerings.

Cutting down the loosefeed

I've decided to cut down on the amount of loosefeed. I will still catapult bait every couple of minutes, but I will use half as many pellets as I was using previously. This makes the fish compete even more for the feed, as hopefully there will be more fish in

my swim than falling trout pellets.

This style of fishing requires stronger tackle, simply because the bites can be extremely violent. A fish has to lunge at the bait before the next fish gets it. So I am using a top three kit threaded with eight feet of number ten elastic, as opposed to a number eight when fishing a bait on the bottom.

My pole float is different, too. It is an extremely buoyant and strong dibber pattern, a Preston Innovations' Tyson, which won't be dragged under by the extra weight of my suspended bait. Let's bait the hook and see happens.

I've fired out a few more pellets and there are still swirls caused by fish darting around just beneath the surface. On goes another slither of drenched meat and out goes the rig.

▲ *Yet another carp falls to Bob's perfectly presented bait meat.*

At present, the hook is set three feet deep with only three number eight shot spread down the line. This provides a slow, steady fall of the hookbait through the shoal of frantically feeding fish.

Well, it isn't too long before I get my first bite. The meat must have been only inches beneath the surface and they really are feeding well. This particular fish is certainly giving me the major run-around – it's screaming off in all directions, but luckily I have it under control quite quickly, breaking down to the fifth section, piling on the pressure all the time. Soon the fish safe in my keepnet, my hook is re-baited and within seconds is falling through the shoal again. Fishing up-in-the-water for carp can be fast and furious, as you will find out in the next pages.

▼ *After only an hour of continual feeding, Bob tempts the carp to the surface.*

Keep it up!

Y ou have to be on the ball to keep a shoal of hungry carp interested,
as Bob proves in the final part of this carp section

I love it when you can catch up-in-the-water. It gives you a great sense of achievement as you have gradually worked the fish in your swim into a feeding frenzy. All that is left is for you to keep the bait going in and bag-up those fish!

Summer is the best time to give this deadly and frantic style of fishing a try. The water is at its warmest, the fish have finished spawning and are always on the look-out for food. Although on these pages I am fishing solely for carp, you can just as easily fish the same tactics for stillwater chub, roach and rudd, but you will need to alter your feed bait to either hemp, caster or maggot. That's enough rambling, let's get back to catching some more 'pasties'.

Although the shoal of carp in my peg are feeding like there's no tomorrow, I still have to fish cunningly in order to catch them. I have found the best way to trick the carp into taking my bait is to make sure my hookbait falls at the same time and at the same speed as my loosefeed offerings.

Difficult to master method

It's no good allowing your bait to remain motionless at mid-depth because it looks totally unnatural just hanging there. You may get a bite fishing like this, but you certainly won't bag-up. The method I am adopting to catch these fish up-in-the-water is a little difficult to master as you need to be both co-ordinated and competent at loosefeeding while holding a pole.

I actually ship my baited rig out and hold it high above the feeding area, ensuring the hookbait does not enter the water. Now for the complicated part! Immediately after catapulting a few trout pellets into my swim I move my pole and swing my rig to the right. Then, when the rig straightens out, I swing the pole down and to the

◀ *Bob holding up the results of a successful session.*

left. This lays the rig neatly and in a straight line on the water's surface.

The shirt-button style shotting pattern forces my Nice 'n' Spicy meat bait through the water at the same speed as my loosefed pellets. This, to the carp, looks completely natural and they normally accept the bait without any hesitation at all.

Best method yet

There are other ways to get your rig into the water, but I have found this way to be the best yet, simply because the rig has straightened out before it begins to drop through the water and hence causes no tangles. Dropping the rig vertically into the water can cause problems. You may experience tangles and also missed bites as the rig will be almost looped over itself as it falls through the first two feet of water.

If my rig settles and the hookbait reaches the end of its descent without a bite I simply catapult a few more trout pellets into the swim, lift the pole tip so my bait rises and then allow my hookbait to fall through the feeding fish once more.

So far this method has accounted for six carp here with plenty more to come. Every time I loosefeed I see swirls on the water surface caused by carp darting around looking for more food. This is a great sign as it proves there is a substantial amount of fish in my swim all competing for the same food. Let's go for number seven.

Again I've baited my hook with another slither of drenched luncheon meat and shipped out ready to lay the rig on the water's surface. Out goes another pouchful of trout pellets, quickly followed by my rig.

For a split second my Preston Innovations' Tyson dibber lays flat on the surface. It quickly cocks as the first shot pulls on the float's short stem and vanishes subsurface.

On this occasion I needn't strike as the fish has obviously realised it has been hooked and bolts away, pulling plenty of elastic from the pole tip.

Pressure on the fish

I've reacted to the situation quickly, applying plenty of pressure on the fish straight away. This feels like the biggest carp of the session. It really is going well. Again, my two spare sections set-up behind me are put to good use as the carp surges directly away from me and to my right.

I'm holding the pole high, putting a tremendous amount of pressure on the fish. The pole I'm using, a Browning Nickel Reflex, has very strong sections – even when playing large, powerful fish only the three tip sections bend.

This fish really is giving me the run-around. I've been playing it for about 30 seconds now

STEP ONE

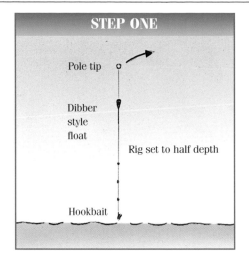

▲ Hold the rig over your feeding zone, catapult loosefeed and move your pole to the right.

STEP TWO

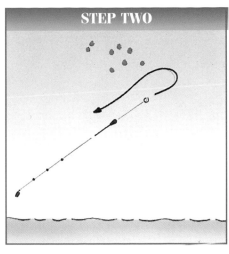

▲ With a smooth but sharp action, whip the pole tip round and to the left.

STEP THREE

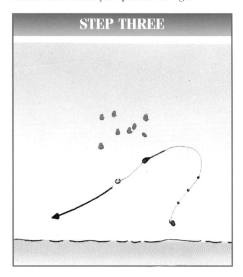

▲ Continue moving the pole tip to the left, but drop slightly towards the water surface.

STEP FOUR

▲ As the rig hits the surface, lift the pole tip a little, keeping a tight line between tip and float.

STEP FIVE

▲ Your hookbait will fall through the water at the same speed as your loosefeed items.

STEP SIX

▲ Nearby carp will chase loosefeed as it falls, and readily accept your naturally presented bait.

◀ A strong pole is a must when you go carp fishing, and the Browning that Bob is using is tough enough to take on the hardest-fighting carp there is.

▼ The beaming smile says it all – well over 60lb of prime, pristine condition, hard-fighting carp.

and it's showing no signs of slowing.

Now's the time to make a decision. I either continue playing the carp until it's in the net and then turn my attention to my swim once more, or I could feed my swim while playing the carp.

The latter makes more sense, simply because I could be playing the carp for a fairly long time, and in that time the carp searching around for more feed could lose interest and swim off elsewhere.

Catapult at the ready

My catapult is always at the ready, perched on the side of my baitwaiter. All I have to do is simply pick out a few pellets, drop them into the cup and pick the catapult up with my left hand. The I just have to fire the baits over my 10-metre line.

I do this by holding both the catapult pouch and pole in my right hand and push the catapult body forward and release the pouch. It's as simple as that. My two inside lines need feeding as well, so out go a few more grains of sweetcorn, flicked in by hand.

When feeding a line while playing a fish you must take care so as not to jerk the pole tip around as you flick the baits out or release the pouch. Any jerky movements on the pole tip could pull the hook from the fish's mouth. Eventually the fish tires, I have a chance to break my pole down to the fifth section and gently glide the fish over my landing net under the largest fish of the day - a lovely, 6 lb mirror carp.

Now I think it's time to try out both my inside lines to see if they hold any fish. I already have a rig set-up for

these two lines. It is set upon a number 12 elastic threaded through three sections. The float is a Preston Innovation's Brio and my shot is set shirt button style down the mainline. On goes a grain of sweetcorn onto the size 14 hook and the rig is flicked out into the swim on my left.

The next fish

Two minutes pass and there's no sign of any life - time to try the swim on my right, but I still have to loosefeed my 10-metre line first. If you want a good day's fishing you must always think about the next fish. If you do, there's every chance you will bag-up!

On the first put-in my float trembles as a fish rubs against my mainline. Things are looking up!

The float bobs, rises a little as the bottom-most shot lifts off the bottom, and gently

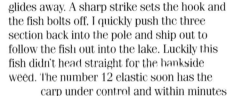

▲ *Bob loosefeeds his 10-metre line even while playing fish, so as not to lose the fish's interest.*

▼ *Sweetcorn was the bait to produce the best carp of the day.*

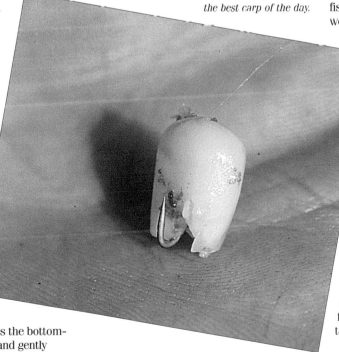

glides away. A sharp strike sets the hook and the fish bolts off. I quickly push the three section back into the pole and ship out to follow the fish out into the lake. Luckily this fish didn't head straight for the bankside weed. The number 12 elastic soon has the carp under control and within minutes it is unhooked and in my keepnet. This really is great fishing!

I've decided to rest my inside line for a short while and go back to my up-in-the-water rig. Five consecutive put-ins produce four healthy carp and my weight certainly is building up.

I decide to call it a day after five frantic hours' fishing. All three of my lines have produced fish, but by far the most productive has been my shallow, 10 metre swim. Here the action has been fantastic - I couldn't catch the carp fast enough.

By my reckoning I have had managed to take over 60 lb of prime, hard-fighting carp and a great day's fishing by anyone's standards. Get your rigs correctly balanced, feed continually and fish confidently and you too could do the same.

All I have to do now is wish you good luck!

Tipped for the top!

When it comes to pole fishing, you'd be hard pressed to find a better tutor than triple world-champion Bob. Here's his 50-tip rundown for world-class performance

1 Make the right choice

Never, under any circumstances, buy a new pole without trying it out first. Persuade the tackle shop staff to allow you to set the pole up to its fullest length before parting with your well-earned cash.

2 Don't be blinkered

There are so many poles available nowadays that you would be silly to buy the first one you see. Many tackle shops offer great deals and huge discounts which may allow you to purchase a longer, lighter and stiffer pole than you would expect. Shop around and you will be pleasantly surprised.

3 What about spares?

Make sure the pole you are buying comes with at least one spare top three kit. Spare kits give you the freedom to tackle a wide variety of fish with different strength elastics and various rigs without having to waste valuable fishing time threading new elastic and attaching further rigs.

4 Cut your losses

Take great care when cutting down your tip section when fitting your external or internal PTFE bush. Start by aiming to make your first cut a little short of where you really expect the bush to fit, and then you can continue cutting the pole tip down, an inch or so at a time, until the bush fits perfectly.

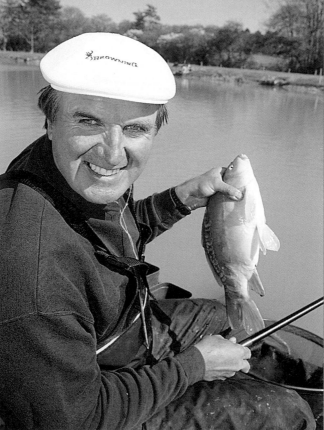

▲ *Is your pole strong enough to handle carp?*

5 What is it for?

Think long and hard about the style of fishing you intend to pursue before purchasing your first pole. If you wish to tackle carp you must buy a pole that is capable of stopping these hard-fighting fish. If you wish to start match fishing, opt for a stiff, lightweight pole which you could use for long periods at 11 or 12.5 metres.

6 How many sections?

Whichever elastic you are using, make sure it is threaded through the correct amount of pole sections. Elastic numbers one and two should be set inside the tip section only. Numbers three to six should be placed through both the tip and second section. All other grades of elastic should be threaded through the first three sections.

7 Don't be tight

Ensure your PTFE bush is the right size. Your elastic should pass through the bush freely, but not to such an extent that there is a wide gap between elastic and bush, as this will allow dirt, water and other nasties entering the tip section.

8 Rig it right

Always match the correct grade of elastic to the species you are targeting. Use either numbers one, two or three for the likes of bleak, gudgeon, small roach and perch. Try three, four or five for quality roach, perch, skimmers and small chub. For tench, bream, chub and eel use numbers six or eight, and for carp, barbel and big tench select grades ten and above.

9 On the wire

Avoid pole floats having wire tips/bristles as they are extremely difficult to shot correctly and so fine they are almost impossible to spot at a distance. They are best left to the professionals!

10 Choose the right stem

Match the float stem to your desired presentation. If you want your bait presented hard on the bottom, opt for a float having a stable wire stem. If you are fishing on the drop, use a float having a more buoyant stem such as either glass fibre or carbon.

11 It's a balancing act

Get your pole roller positioned correctly. Simply set your pole up to the desired length, sit on your box and push the pole back towards dry land. When you can balance the pole in one hand, put the pole down on the bank and place your roller at the end of your pole. Now, when the pole comes off the roller, it will be perfectly balanced, making shipping out so much easier.

▼ *A correctly-positioned pole roller will make shipping out so much smoother.*

12 Mix and match

Always match your mainline and hooklength to the elastic you are using. Lines with diameters between 0.05mm and 0.08mm are best suited to numbers one and two elastic. Lines between 0.08mm and 0.10mm are best matched to elastics three and four. Lines from 0.10mm through to 0.12mm should be used with grades five and six. For grade eight and ten use 0.12mm and 0.13mm lines, and for number 12 elastic and above, use no finer than 0.13mm line.

13 Be careful!

Whether you are buying a brand-new pole or a second-hand one, you must check all the joints and sections carefully. The ends of every section need to be smooth and free from any hairline fractures. Check the wall strength of each section, particularly numbers three, four and five, by squeezing them gently. These three sections are the most likely ones to break.

14 Be selective

Make sure that you select the right pole float to suit the fishing conditions. If you are fishing a river, opt for a body-up pattern which will ride the flowing water well. Deep stillwaters require a body-down, or pear-shaped float, which provides a stable, stationary presentation. Small, slender, oval floats are really best suited to situations such as canals, shallow stillwaters and sluggish rivers.

15 Three's best

Remember that it is always worthwhile using three small strips of silicone tubing for attaching your pole float to the mainline. Using these strips helps to ensure that the float does not slip down the line when you are playing fish. Don't forget too, that the bottom-most silicone strip should overlap the float's stem by a small amount, as this minimises the chances that your rig will get tangled.

◀ Match your mainline and hooklength to the elastic you are using.

20 Size does matter

Matching hook size to bait puts more fish in your net, and that's a fact. For the likes of maggot and casters, use fine wire hooks between sizes 22 and 18. For hemp a fine wire, wide gape size 20 or 18 hook is ideal. Punched bread requires a lightweight, long shank hook with a curved-in point. Sizes 18 or 20 are ideal for bread. Paste is totally different. You can mould this around the hook, so you can get away with any size from an 18 through to a size eight. If carp are the quarry, use a hook made from a strong wire.

16 On reflection

Look carefully at the water's surface before selecting your pole rig. If the water is shaded and dark, use a yellow-tipped float. If it reflects the sky and is almost white, go for a black-tipped float. If there are ripples and distorted, multi-coloured reflections, your best choice would be a red-tipped float.

17 Double up

Whether you are a match angler or a pleasure angler, it is always worthwhile making up at least two of every rig. If you do break the rig on a fish or snag, or make a mistake and the rig tangles, you can always resort to your second rig within seconds.

18 Make a note

When making up your rigs, it helps to mark the side of your winder with the relevant information. Write, in a fine permanent marker pen, the rig length, the mainline breaking strain and diameter, the weight of the float, hook size and pattern.

19 Sit up straight

Holding a pole for long durations can lead to backache, but only if you haven't positioned your seatbox correctly. Try to adjust your seat height so that your feet are flat to the floor and your thighs are parallel to the horizon. In this position you can steady your pole by pressing the butt section onto your thigh with your forearm.

21 Be prepared

Pole fishing for carp requires strong, stout tackle and fast reflexes. Carp will often bolt after they have been hooked, so it makes sense to be prepared. Have at least two spare butt sections set up behind you, ready to add at any moment, if a fish heads directly away from you.

22 Think small

Shotting pole floats correctly requires the tiniest of shot. Forget about BBs, AAAs and SSGs – we're talking number 8, 9, 10, 11, 12 and even number 13. These tiny shot enable even the finest pole float bristles to be dotted down so they register even slight knocks on the bait.

23 Select the right hook

The delicate floats, tiny shot and fine lines used in pole fishing all combine to make perfect presentations, which trick a lot of fish into taking the bait. This can quickly be ruined simply by using the wrong hook. Avoid thick, 'heavy', eyed hooks, especially when fishing fine for the likes of bream, roach and skimmers, and opt for spade-end hooks. They are generally finer and lighter, so offer better hookbait presentation.

24 Don't forget

It has been said a million times before, but you must plumb the depth of your swim carefully on every single session. You will be able to locate any ledges, holes, bars and dropoffs, which may hold plenty of fish.

▼ Squeezing the walls of each section will reveal any weak spots in the construction.

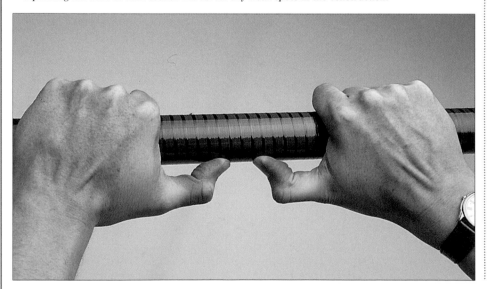

25 Hit the bull's eye

You will not find a more accurate device for loosefeeding or introducing small balls of groundbait than a pole cup. This is a brilliant little invention that is perfect for laying down a bed of feed at the start of your session.

26 Get it covered

Take a leaf out of the match angler's handbook and tie your hooks at home. Under these circumstances you are not rushed, you have everything to hand and you can prepare a vast array of hook and hooklength combinations, sufficient to cover all eventualities.

27 Make your mark

Once you have plumbed the depth, it is vitally important to mark the point at which your float lies. There are many ways to do this, but I have my marker pen idea to be the simplest. All you do is colour your line with a permanent pen, just above the pole float's eye.

28 Line them up

If you want to keep a steady run of fish coming to your net, you must feed two or more areas regularly. Three or four maggots, casters, grains of hemp or sweetcorn, introduced every couple of minutes, will keep plenty of fish interested throughout the day. If one area is devoid of fish, you can always try another area, and so on.

29 Drop in upstream

When fishing a bulk shot or olivette rig over a bed of groundbait, it is always best to swing your hookbait upstream of the mix when putting in. This ensures that your hookbait reaches the bottom, well before it rides over the groundbait mix, and within reach of any fish sitting directly over the groundbait.

30 Make good contact

When pole fishing it is necessary to strike with a firm, but controlled lift, so as to set the hook

correctly into the fish's mouth. This is more so when fishing lighter elastics which haven't the power to push a hook home.

31 Try the margins

Just because your pole is 11, 12.5 or 14 metres, it doesn't mean you always have to fish at this length. Many species, including carp and tench, can be found close to your feet, in the margins.

32 It's common sense

Before you head off to your nearest carp pit, sweetcorn, paste and luncheon meat in hand, ask yourself this question – is my pole up to it? If you don't think it is, then you are better off using a rod and line. There's no point in breaking your valuable pole for the sake of one fish.

▲ Be ready to add spare sections if a fish bolts.

33 Smooth is best

Lubricating your elastic before every session should be a second-nature habit, but if it isn't, just slide out your pole bung and squirt lubricant down the tip sections of your pole. This ensures that your elastic runs freely and smoothly from the pole tip.

34 Pile on the pressure

Remember that you have to keep constant pressure on hooked carp at all times. Try to get as much elastic out of your pole as possible, in order to tire the fish out. If you don't, you could be playing the fish for hours!

◀ *Have plenty of ready-tied hooks to hand.*

35 Break down correctly

When breaking your pole down when landing fish, remember to take into account the stretched elastic. When landing carp, you may have to break your pole two or even three sections further down than you would when re-baiting the hook.

36 Keep feeding

A good, consistent match angler will always think about the next fish, even when one's on the end of the line. This is more so when carp fishing, as it may take a few minutes to get a fair-sized carp to the bank. If this is the case, it is worthwhile feeding your line at least once while playing the fish, to keep the rest of the shoal interested.

37 Get control

Once you have hooked into a fish and your elastic begins to slide from the pole tip, get the fish under control as quickly as you possibly can. Under no circumstances should you allow the fish to swim back into your loosefeed area, for fear of it flashing around – if so, it will scare the rest of the shoal.

38 Keep on the move

When presenting a bait at mid-depth with a strung-out shotting pattern, you must always keep your bait on the move. Gently lay the rig on the surface and allow the bait to fall at the same time as your loosefeed. Once it reaches the end of its descent, lift the bait out of the water and lay the rig on the surface again.

39 Winding up

When making your own rigs, it is imperative that you purchase the right sized winders to house your pole floats. They need to be long enough to enable the float to sit inside, and wide and deep enough to accommodate the float's body without crushing it.

40 Change tactics

If you are getting a lot of line bites when presenting a bait on the bottom, the fish in your swim may have moved up-in-the-water. If this is the case, change your rig to a dibber pattern, set at around half-depth with tiny, strung out shot, and try presenting your bait on the drop. The dibber float's extra-buoyant tip won't be pulled under with the weight of your settling bait.

41 Don't get snagged

Step up a grade or two of elastic when presenting your bait tight to weeds. This will give the extra 'stopping power' required to ensure larger fish do not get snagged or lost.

42 Play safe

Don't jerk your pole around or move the tip from one side of your body to the other while playing fish. This widens the hole caused by the hook, eventually weakening its hold. This is a sure recipe for disaster, especially when you are using barbless hooks.

43 Hold it

Get used to holding your pole, as opposed to sitting on it or leaving it in a rest. Bites are often very quick, especially from smaller fish, so you need to be ready at all times. If you aren't holding your pole you will miss many bites.

◀ *Make sure you get to grips with feeding while holding your pole.*

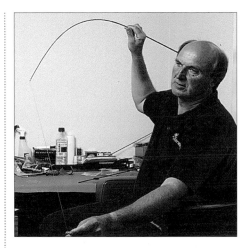

▲ Ensure your elastic slides back smoothly.

47 Run it through

After plumbing the depth on a river swim, always run your rig through the swim with a bare hook. This will indicate any underwater snags, as the float will drag under. You will now know to avoid these snags.

48 Lean forward

If you regularly loosefeed using a clip-on pole pot, always lean forward with the pole pushed out as far as possible. This is because the pot normally needs to be positioned some way down the pole's tip section. Now you can easily manoeuvre your float over your loosefeed.

49 A tense time

Take time out to tension your elastic correctly, as this could make all the difference when playing fish. A correctly-tensioned elastic should always slide back inside the pole when stretched after playing a fish. It should return smoothly and steadily, not snap back sharply.

50 Watch out!

Take great care when fishing venues having a path close to the bankside. You may need to position your pole roller at 90 degrees to the bank, to avoid blocking the way of passing cyclists and pedestrians.

44 Carry spares

If you break your elastic during a session, have the equipment to fix it. Always carry some spare elastic, connectors, a bung, and the most important item of all – a diamond eye threader.

45 Use a marker

Although poles allow you to place your bait in exactly the right position every put-in, you should still use a far bank marker. Select a tree, bush, gate, house, etc and use your marker as a guide when positioning your float.

46 Take care

Look up before you fish. Do not, under any circumstances, fish underneath or close to overhead power lines. There have been far too many deaths through electrocution.

◀ Make sure your winders are the right size to house your pole floats.

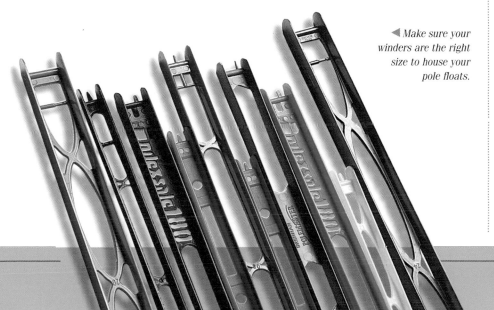

Bob's Question & Answer
Pole fishing browser

There are hours of useful reading here, and if you follow Bob's advice, you'll improve your catch record no end! Read on and enjoy.

The way to start

Q I would like to start pole fishing but I don't know whether to buy a cheap new pole or a second-hand one of better quality. If I go for the second-hand one what should I look out for when checking its condition?

A The first thing to look for in a second-hand pole is the condition of the third and fourth joints. These joints get the most wear and tear as they are the most favourable unshipping areas for all anglers. Take a close look at them and check there are no cracks, the walls of the sections are still strong and intact and there are no deep scratches. If they are in good condition you know the pole has not been used much.

You should then put the pole together at its fullest length and pretend to strike, quite powerfully, into a fish. If there are any hairline fractures along the pole's length it will crack. If the pole seems intact and in good condition my advice is to buy it, as you will get a better performing pole than a new one of the same price.

Caring for your pole

Q I am a 12-year-old who has just recently bought a pole. Please could you tell me the best way to look after it and what cleaning materials should I use?

A All you have to do is wipe the pole clean with either clean water or a little bit of diluted washing-up liquid. Do not use any harsh abrasive cleaners that are in your mother's cupboards as these will damage the pole. Always dry your pole or rods before storing them, as water will seep into the varnish or joint sections, eventually weakening them.

Feeding worms

Q I find it difficult to feed worms by hand or catapult when pole-fishing. Is there an easier and more accurate way of loosefeeding worms into my swim?

A There is only one way to loosefeed worms with any degree of accuracy and that is to use a pole cup.

► *Pole cup*

All you do is clip the pole cup to the tip of your pole and place the worm inside it. Then, very gently, ship the pole out until the cup is hovering above the desired area and tip the contents into the water. Now you have fed the swim and you can fish directly over the top of your feed. Worms aren't the only feed you can introduce by a pole cup, you can use them for anything, like maggots, casters, corn or even small balls of groundbait.

Breaking the elastic

Q When pole fishing for the first time recently I got snagged on the bottom. I tried to free my line but I over-stretched the elastic which broke just above the line connector. Can I simply re-use this elastic or is it best to renew it?

A I would advise you to replace the elastic as it sounds as though you have stretched your elastic to its limit and it would therefore be too weak. You should change your elastic regularly anyway, especially if you have played some big fish on it.

Always bear in mind that all rubber products deteriorate in time. Pole elastic will need close inspection every time you go fishing to avoid any nasty little accidents when playing fish.

River pole

Q I've just bought my first pole and find it quite comfortable to use on local pools, but now I would like to use it on the River Severn. Are there any special methods for pole fishing on a river that are different to those used on stillwater fishing?

A Pole fishing a river is quite difficult. To combat the flow you will need a longer length of line between your pole tip and the float to allow the float to drift downstream. It will be extremely difficult for anyone, especially a newcomer, to fish most stretches of the River Severn as it has a fast flow. Select a deeper peg or one on a corner as the flow will be slower and you will be able to control your tackle that bit easier. You

▶ *A typical whip catch.*

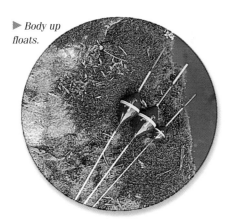

▶ *Body up floats.*

will also have to change rigs and use a float with a 'body up' design. These floats have pear-shaped bodies with the wider part at the top. Experiment with shotting patterns to determine which one works best for you and the fish.

Attaching rigs

Q **I have just bought a new whip but I don't know how to attach any of my rigs to the fine tip. Can you tell me how it's done?**

A The easiest way would be to buy a flick tip connector from your local tackle shop These tiny plastic connectors simply glue to the end of your whip and incorporate a sliding lock mechanism onto which you can clip your rig.

Alternatively you could use two pieces of thin silicone tubing. To do this cut two half inch strips, one should be thread onto your rig's mainline, the other should

be glued two to three inches from the end of your whip tip. Form a two inch loop in the end of your rig mainline and push the mainline through this loop. In doing this another loop is formed. Thread the larger loop over the whip's tip and silicone. Now thread the mainline silicone over the tip of the whip until half an inch protrudes from the end of the carbon and pull the mainline tight. The rig is now totally secure.

Pole or whip?

Q **I would love either a pole or whip for my next birthday, but I don't know the difference between the two. Which of these alternatives do you think I would be best spending my money on?**

A The main difference between poles and whips are that poles are equipped with elastic, whips are not. This means that poles can cope with larger fish provided they are equipped with stronger elastic.

Poles also can be bought anything up to 16 metres in length, the longest whip is about 8 metres. Whips are designed for catching very small fish such as perch and gudgeon at speed.

They have a very thin 'flick-tip' at the top of the pole which absorbs the fight of the small fish. If I were you I would invest in a pole as they are a lot more versatile. Take a good look at the opening section of this book to see exactly the sort of thing that you should be looking for when you take all your money along to the tackle shop!

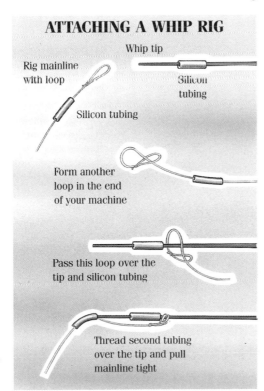

ATTACHING A WHIP RIG

Whip tip

Rig mainline with loop

Silicon tubing

Silicon tubing

Form another loop in the end of your machine

Pass this loop over the tip and silicon tubing

Thread second tubing over the tip and pull mainline tight

Ready-made or D-I-Y?

Q **I have recently bought a pole and I've wondered if it would be better buying ready-made rigs at around £2.50 or buying a pack of pole floats and making my own rigs. Which do you think is best?**

A Ready-made rigs are by far the easiest option and are fine for a great deal of situations. I would recommend buying a couple at least as then you can get a good idea of how pole rigs are set-up. But, in the long term, I suggest buying a set of pole floats, good low diameter hi-tech line, a selection of tiny shot, say numbers 10 - 13, and a wide selection of hooks. You will now be able to set-up a wider variety of rigs all for different set-ups.

I always make-up at least two of each rig as then you have a quick replacement if a fish, snag or accident breaks you. You will learn a whole lot more making-up your own rigs as you can experiment with many different styles. Also, it is great fun making up your own rigs, and it's even better catching fish on them.

Storage answers

Q **I hear of elastic being threaded through the top three or even four sections of a pole but, if this is so, how do you break down the pole for storage?**

A For a start I would never recommend any angler elasticate four sections of their pole. Three sections are more than enough, especially with today's advanced elastics. To solve the problem of storage all you need to do is get yourself an elastic band, a pole winder and an empty

Q&A Pole fishing browser

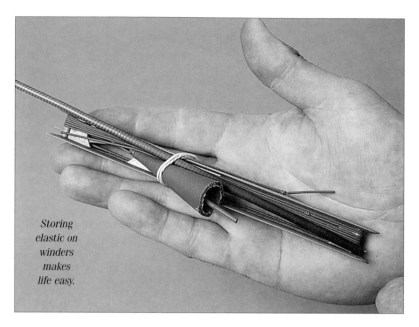

Storing elastic on winders makes life easy.

tube the same length as your tip section. Simply remove the bung from your third section, pull the elastic from within the pole until the tip section slides out. Hold the bung against the pole winder and wrap your elastic round it until you reach the tip section of your pole. Simply clip the winder to the pole section using the elastic band and store the whole lot in the tube.

Every time you need to use the pole, unravel the elastic and drop the tip section into the second and third sections until the bung locks in place.

Mind the joggers!

Q I've bought a new pole roller but as I fish a lot of canals I find its use is more limited than I expected. With so many joggers, walkers and cyclists also using the towpath it is proving very difficult to unship my pole, especially when I am playing a decent sized fish. Have you any ideas as what I can do?

A Whatever you do, don't give up fishing your canal stretch just because of pedestrians and the like; we all have to share the facilities, with give and take on both sides. In fact, there is a solution to your problem; it takes a little practice but will save you a damaged pole. All you do is place the roller on either your left or your right, whatever you feel most comfortable with, making sure that it is between the towpath and the water's edge.

For argument's sake let's say you'd prefer the pole roller on your right. When you hook into a fish, gradually ease it to the left, and away from the shoal. Now you can use your elastic to tire the fish out in the canal's deeper central track. When the fish is almost ready, try to ease it further to the left so that you can rest the pole on the roller and start the unshipping process. In this way your pole lies parallel to the towpath and out of harm's way from all those joggers and bikers.

Feeder and pole

Q I was surprised to see an angler fishing a feeder in conjunction with his pole recently, though I noticed that he caught quite a few fish like this, so now I would like to give it a try. What elastic and line should I use for this method?

A Well, whatever type you choose, groundbait or maggot feeder, your rig will be a little heavier than usual, especially if you hook into a good sized fish also. I would recommend you step up to a No5 elastic with at least 0.12mm mainline.

On its day the pole fished in conjunction with a feeder is absolutely deadly and I would advise anyone to try it. All you do is tie on a feeder link of around two inches to your mainline using a four-turn waterknot. Your tail, including hooklength, should be around 12 inches long on a stillwater, two feet on a running water.

You may have to add a shot midway along the tail if the water is flowing fast to keep line laying close to the bottom. Bites are indicated using a float set to the correct depth.

Slipping elastic

Q I have been having problems with the elastic in the tip of my pole. Every time I hook a decent sized fish the elastic slips out the pole as usual but around a foot is left hanging from the tip afterwards. How can I prevent this happening?

A There are two reasons why this could be happening. The first, and simplest is that your elastic isn't set under enough tension. You should remove the old elastic and replace with new elastic. Always remember, your new elastic may need adjusting after the first couple of visits.

The second fault may be in the diameter of your bush. If it is too tight your elastic will not slip back inside your pole. Have a close look at your elastic and bush. There should be a minute gap between the two. If there is not then replace the bush with another one of a wider diameter.

◄ *Lay tackle upstream of groundbait.*

Upstream or downstream?

Q I am a newcomer to pole fishing and could do with a little help. When fishing a river should I lay my terminal tackle upstream or downstream of my float?

A This is a very good question. The answer depends upon the terminal tackle, your shotting pattern and feed. If you are fishing over groundbait with a heavy rig incorporating an olivette you should lay your baited hook upstream of your float. This will allow your hookbait to hit the bottom just before it reaches your groundbait. Now your rig is ready to accept bites from fish as soon as it passes over the feed area.

If you are loosefeeding and fishing on-the-drop you would be best laying your baited hook downstream of the float. This allows your baited hook to act naturally in the flow, dropping at the same speed and in the same direction as your loosefeed. If you were to lay your hook upstream of the float the flow may cause your mainline to arc unnaturally, and occasionally tangle.

Playing fish

Q I have recently been given an eight metre pole. As I usually fish with rod and line I know how to play the fish on a running line, but how do I play a fish when using a pole?

A Playing a fish on the pole is, believe it or not, a whole lot easier than playing a fish with normal rod and line tactics. This is purely because the design of the pole means that the elastic within it does all the work for you. It compensates for your winding and backwinding as it stretches backwards and forwards from the tip of your pole.

When you strike into a fish, slowly drag it away from the feeding shoal. Now try to keep the pole tip above the fish at all times, while letting your elastic do the work for you.

Only when you start to feel the fish begin to slow down and tire should you start the unshipping process. Take the pole apart as smoothly and as carefully as you can while making sure you are keeping the elastic under tension. If you follow these simple steps you should land all your fish.

Line length

Q Please explain what is the ideal length of line between the float and pole tip and what determines it?

A There really is no ideal length of line between pole tip and float, it depends entirely upon the venue you are fishing and conditions.

If I am fishing a stillwater, which is coloured, and the conditions are good I would aim to have about two to three feet of line between pole and float. If I'm fishing the same stillwater and there's a wind blowing straight towards me I would aim to have as little as 12 inches of line between pole and float to prevent the float drifting. If I am fishing a flowing venue the ideal length of line would be between two and three metres. This gives enough spare line to allow the float to trot through the swim and therefore catch fish that are shying away from the feed area.

Another reason to use a longer line between pole and float is when fishing clear venues. This prevents the pole's tip hanging close to the float and possibly spooking the fish.

Try to keep your pole tip above the fish at all times and let your elastic do the work for you.

Q&A Pole fishing browser

Accurate loosefeeding

Q If I have my pole in a rest I can catapult my loosefeed very accurately. However, when I attempt to loosefeed while balancing the pole the results are disastrous. Have you any tips on how to hold a pole and loosefeed accurately at the same time?

A First of all, if your pole is not too heavy, place it across your knee. Now you should trap the pole securely using the flat part of your forearm. Press down on the pole section with enough pressure to lock it in place. By applying slightly more pressure to the elbow you can raise the pole tip, slightly more pressure from the wrist will lower the tip. Then, to feed accurately, you should hold the catapult pouch with the same hand that is pressing down on the pole. You should hold the catapult in your other hand.

Now this is the most important part. To loosefeed in this position push the catapult away from the pouch. In effect, you are using the catapult in reverse, pushing the catapult away from the pouch and not pulling the pouch away from the catapult as you would when feeding a waggler line, for example. It does take a little practice but is very accurate and a technique that comes as second nature in time.

Locked together

Q Just recently the fourth and fifth section of my 11 metre pole locked together. I've tried twisting and pulling at the sections and have even tried WD40. How do I get them apart and prevent this happening again?

A The method I always use to release any stuck joints requires three people and has always worked for me. First, place two of the people at both ends of the stuck joints. The third person should be positioned at the point where

the joints are stuck. While the two are pulling at the pole sections the other should gently, and I stress gently, be tapping the stuck area with the flat of the hand, in a similar way to a gentle karate chop. It only requires the two stuck sections to move a millimetre and you should quickly be able to free the joints. To stop this happening in future make sure you assemble your pole, or store it away, when it is completely dry. This goes for all your tackle.

Off the hook

Q I have a lot of problems bumping small fish off the hook when unshipping my pole. Is there a technique to prevent this?

A I should think the problem lies with your elastic. It sounds as though it is too strong for the size of fish you are catching. Try rigging your pole with say a number one or two elastic through only one section coupled with plenty of lubricant. This softer set-up will cushion the fight of even the smallest fish and therefore prevent any fish being bumped off during the unshipping process. Also, any jerky movements will be absorbed by the elasic. This may seem a little too light, but recently I was fishing a match using a similar set-up. I was catching a good run of roach when suddenly a 4lb tench took the bait. I still got the fish in, but it took a little longer than the roach I was catching previously. So, with this in mind you can still catch larger fish and not bump smaller ones. Use barbed hooks rather than barbless versions as they do offer better holding power.

Metal advice

Q I would like to make my own pole floats. Can you tell me what metal to use and where I could obtain it?

A I know that Future produce packs of stainless steel wire used in the pole float making process. Your local tackle shop should be able to get you a pack of these if you ask them, failing that give Future a ring direct on 0181 5993831. Quite frankly though, the quality of their own floats and many others on the market are so good and they're so cheap that it really isn't worth spending all that time making your own floats. You might as well save time and buy ready made floats. If I were you I'd stick to making wagglers and stick floats.

Attaching method

Q I understand there is a method of attaching your rig to elastic without using a Stonfo connector. How is this done?

A Simply thread a short length of silicone over the end of your elastic and tie a small, one inch loop in the end of your elastic. Pull tight so the elastic digs into itself and the knot is secure. You will then have a loop and a short length of surplus elastic. Cut the surplus until it is around an eighth of an inch long and then cut the loop in half and trim both ends until they are an eighth of an inch long too. Tie, using a double overhand knot, a two inch loop in the end of your mainline.

Now tie another tiny loop in the end of the first so the end of your mainline resembles a small figure of eight. Now pass your mainline through the largest loop formed, as in the diagram, and pass your elastic through the loop you have just formed.

Now pull your mainline until it grips tight, behind your elastic knot. All that's left is to pass the silicone over the mainline knot and elastic knot to neaten the end product and there you have it.

Loose joints

Q Some of the joints on my pole are loose and need building up. Can you recommend the best product to use and how best to use it?

A Browning used to make their own Pole Joint Protector spray that I have used on all of my poles. It comes in an aerosol form and is very good indeed. It allows you to quickly and gradually build up a layer of carbon onto your joints with the minimum of fuss.

Maver also make a good quality spray called Carbon Graphite which costs around £6. Instructions are printed on the can of each spray and should be followed to the word. Always make sure

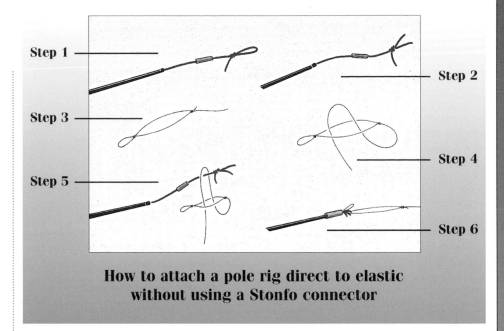

How to attach a pole rig direct to elastic without using a Stonfo connector

Step 1 / Step 2 / Step 3 / Step 4 / Step 5 / Step 6

your pole section to be sprayed is clean, dry and free of dust and dirt before you begin the spraying process.

Alternatively, you could very carefully cut back the section which slides into the next largest section. Using a small junior hacksaw cut off about 1cm, smoothing off the rough edges with fine sandpaper. Check to see if the joint fits correctly; if it is still a little loose try again. Continue this until the pole section fits snugly.

Length and line

Q When you are making up your rigs how long do you have your line? Also, should you put the hooklength onto your rig when you are making it up or leave it off until you begin the session?

A If I am due to fish a competition I would do a little research to find out what kind of venue it is. I ask myself is it a river? If so, how fast does it run? Or is it a stillwater? And lastly, how deep is it? Then I make up two or three rigs according to the information I found.

If the venue is 6ft deep I would always make up my rigs deeper as you can always cut the line down to suit. With this in mind I would make up the rigs to around 9ft long. If it is a river then I would make the rig even longer so I can trot the float through the swim.

In my research I would also find out what species I will be catching and

select a hook to suit. Then I would either attach the hook straight to my mainline or on a hooklength. Then, to finish the rig I always mark the winder with the rig length, mainline and hooklength diameter, float size and lastly hook pattern and size.

Disappearing float

Q I shot my floats in a tank so they sit perfectly in the water. However, when I bait the hook and fish just off the bottom my float disappears. Why is this happening?

A I think that the main reason why your float sinks is probably the size of bait you are using. Pole float tips are very sensitive things and a heavy bait such as a worm, chunk of meat and paste will drag it under. Baits like maggots, casters and bread won't affect the float at all.

You would do best shotting up a float having a thicker cane bristle. These versions offer a little more buoyancy than ultra-thin wire or nylon bristles and can therefore hold a larger bait.

Alternatively you could remove one or two of the smaller shot enabling the float to ride higher in the water. Always bear in mind though, your pre-shotted pole floats won't act the same when you're fishing. You almost always have to add or subtract a shot to make it sit properly anyway. Perhaps tap water's a different density!

Q&A Pole fishing browser

Carp on the surface

Q **Is it possible to pole fish for carp on the surface, using mixers and bread, during the warmer summer months? If so, how is it done and what set-up should I choose?**

A Yes, it is possible but I certainly wouldn't advise it. This is because carp rise to the surface to take floating baits and are therefore looking skywards. They will quickly spot your pole tip, turn tail and totally ignore your bait. I suppose the only solution would be to use a longer than average line between your pole tip and bait in order to alleviate this problem.

In circumstances like this it would be advantageous to use running line instead. This gives you better control over a running fish and there's nothing hovering directly above the fish to spook them too.

Broken pole

Q **Recently I slipped and fell back on my pole breaking the fourth section. What's the best thing to do, either buy a new number four section, buy a universal top four or have the section repaired?**

A The same thing happened to me once while fishing a very important match at Holme Pierrepont. The only way to solve the problem immediately is to push the smaller diameter section back through the thicker end of the larger, forming a telescopic joint. This is only a temporary measure though.

Your best bet, if you can afford it, is to buy a completely new section, specifically designed for your pole. Universal top kits are OK, but they aren't designed for specific poles and therefore aren't balanced accordingly. Repairs cost around £30 to £90. Try North West Pole repairs on 0161 682 3189.

Pole into whip

Q **I have just recently bought a new pole. I would like to know if I could use my old pole, an 8m Daiwa, as a whip. If so, which is the easiest way of doing this?**

A Yes, it is possible to turn your old pole into a whip, all you need is a carbon flick-tip. Take your number two section to your local tackle shop and ask them for a flick-tip to fit.

Now you'll have a whip which can be used from two to eight metres. Bear in mind though, it will not perform as well as a shop-bought whip of the same length. It will be heavy, have a wide butt diameter and will be very difficult to cast. If you wish to take up this style of fishing it would be best buying a whip in the first place.

Housekeeping tips

Q **Having just purchased my first pole, could you give me a few tips on how to care for it after each session. Also, when should I use joint protector?**

A One really important rule to remember when you have finished fishing is to wipe your pole clean and dry before putting it away - this goes for rods too. Any moisture settling in can quickly cause damage,

Use joint protector for extra pole life.

especially to the varnish coating on rods and their whippings. Joint protector is painted onto the pole joints and allowed to dry. It adds extra protection to the areas which receive the most stick and gives them a longer life.

I've also been using the excellent new joint cones for a while now. Drennan, Daiwa and Preston Innovations all produce these simple cheap plastic products which fit snugly inside the thinnest end of each of your pole sections, transforming each joint into a bullet shape. They enable you to put your sections together without crashing joints and cracking carbon.

Tench problems

Q **A local lake near where I live holds an excellent head of medium-sized tench and carp. Every time I hook one of the tench the eye on my pole float comes away from the float body. What's going wrong?**

A Well, the float you are using is probably quite inferior in quality. This is a common occurance though, as the tiny eye screwed into the float's body is so small they often can't get a good enough grip. This has happened to me on a number of occasions leading me to try out a method to prevent it happening again.

Whenever targeting larger fish I thread a small section of silicone over my mainline and then over the float bristle. This takes off the extra tension from the tiny eye and also acts as a double buffer. So, change your pole float to one you have confidence with, try out this method and I guarantee you won't have any more problems like before.

Canal wagglers

Q **Is it viable to use small canal wagglers in conjunction with a pole, or do I always need to use dedicated pole floats?**

A No, you don't always have to use dedicated pole floats at all. Many

▶ *A magnifying glass makes close work much easier on the eye.*

anglers, myself included, use small wagglers. They are great for fishing in a strong wind as the float is attached bottom end only, in the same way as you would when normal waggler fishing, and therefore the line is mostly submerged. This ensures line is not blowing around in the wind, knocking the float around and ultimately affecting presentation.

By far the best situation to use a waggler instead of a pole float is when the wind is blowing along the river, in the opposite direction to the flow. For added stability I often remove one of the shot from the line and replace it around an inch or so above the float. This adds a little extra weight to your line to keep it sub-surface.

By all means use a waggler for your pole fishing, but only when conditions are bad as at all other times a dedicated pole float is best.

Toothed tragedy

Q **When I went fishing for the first time with my new pole I caught a little roach. However, while I was unshipping, a pike took the roach, together with my rig, elastic and the top two sections of my pole. How could I have prevented this happening?**

A Thankfully this has never happened to me before, but I think I know why it happened to you.

First of all your second section must not have been pushed tight enough into your third section. You may also have been playing the roach with your pole tip pointing directly towards the fish, then, when the pike took hold and bolted all the strain was directed onto your bung, which was set either inside your first or second section. When your elastic bottomed out your top two gradually worked free from your pole. You must have also been using a very strong hooklength as this was not broken when the pike took hold.

It is vitally important that you must use a lower breaking strain hooklength than your mainline. This allows you to break the hooklength easily when

accidents such as pike taking your fish, snagging the bottom and tangling in a tree occur.

Springy suggestion

Q **I recently bought a spare top three kit. When I asked my local tackle dealer which elastic I should use, he said to have half No3 and half No6. He said this would be OK for small fish and would cope with larger fish too. Is this set-up advisable?**

A I have never tried this method, although there are many top match anglers that have, and they seem to cope very well with the set-up. My concern is the knot between your two elastics. If it's too large it may stick inside your bush, or it may go through, but not return back.

I suppose that if the bush you are using is of a fairly wide diameter and your strongest elastic is of a fairly low diameter the set-up should be fine. The elastic rig I use is a more simplified version of the same thing.

I have a ten inch loop of 'doubled-up' elastic attached to my bung. This acts as a double buffer when playing larger fish,

when the single length of elastic 'bottoms out' the stronger 'doubled-up' elastic comes into play. Why not keep things simple and use this method instead.

Larger than life

Q **I recently saw a photograph of you sat at your work table. On the table there was a large magnifying glass on a stand. Where did you buy this magnifying glass?**

A Well Bryn, to be honest I can't remember, as it was almost twenty years ago when I bought mine. But don't panic, as I've done a little research and you can still obtain them. The best thing to do is to take a look in your local haberdashery or sewing centre, as you will find them there. Argos sells them, too. Expect to pay between £45 and £60 for the actual magnifying glass with an internal light.

Extra stands and clamps are available as separates for around £15 per item. These allow you to attach your magnifying glass securely to any style of table, rather than relying on its own weighted base.

Why use a pole?

Q **I have been fishing for 18 months now and have noticed that more and more people are using poles. Please can you tell me the advantages and disadvantages of using a pole, as opposed to rod and line.**

A A good question, this one! Well, for a start, the pole isn't always the best option, but it is by far the most efficient one.

This is because the tip of the pole is directly above your float. This ensures you hit more bites as you are in direct contact with the fish. When pole fishing you are also using much finer tackle and your presentation is improved greatly. For example, the elastic takes the strain away from your line so you can get away

Q&A Pole fishing browser

▲ Bob likes his pole fishing.

with lines having as fine a diameter as say 0.06, 0.07 and 0.08mm. This also means you can use much smaller hooks, too. Another plus point for the pole is that when you have a bite and miss it, all you need to do is lift the pole up and drop it down into the swim again, this saves a great deal of time.

The main point against pole fishing is that when the fish are out of range, then other tactics, such as the waggler or feeder must come into play. Like I said before, the pole isn't always the best option, but it is the most efficient.

Rigs for shallows

Q My son pole fishes a small, pacey millstream having a depth of only 22in which holds a good head of roach, tench, chub and perch. Can you recommend a rig for this shallow venue? Also, when he loosefeeds maggot he is plagued by ducks which ruin his swim. How can he feed the swim without attracting the ducks?

A For a start don't let the ducks put you off. Many venues I fish have a lot of ducks moving backwards and

forwards and I am absolutely certain the fish aren't bothered by them in the slightest. Most of the time the ducks move away from the pole's tip anyway, and if they don't, a friendly tap on the head from the pole tip will help them on their way!

If people walking along the venue feed the ducks some bread, then you simply must try it as hookbait, as any free offerings falling through the water will quickly be found and eaten by the fish.

As regards a rig for your 22in deep flowing venue, try one which resembles a stick float and have a long length of line between pole tip and float, as this allows you to trot the float through the swim. You could even try using either a small stick float which was originally designed for use with rod and line, or one of the specially designed pole sticks which are readily available nowadays.

How deep can I fish?

Q When pole fishing, is there a maximum depth you can fish? If so, is it relative to the length of pole you are using?

A Oh yes, there is a maximum depth you can fish and it is slightly shorter that the length of the pole you are using.

There's no way on earth you would be able to fish a venue which is say 30ft deep when you are using a pole which is only 20ft long. You will not be able to ship your rig out, strike into the fish, or net them as there will be far too much slack line.

Obviously your pole has to be a little longer than the depth you are fishing, simply because the pole's tip will bend and your elastic will slide out from the tip under the pressure of a large fish.

But a pole remains by far the best method to use when fishing deep water, as it is easier to control and set-up than a slider rig and is a lot more sensitive than a feeder.

A sticky situation

Q I have been having problems with my pole elastics which I've run through two or more sections. They do not retract properly. There are no obstructions and the tip sections are cut back far enough to accommodate the elastic comfortably. What can I do to solve this problem?

A This is a common occurrence which happens to even the best match anglers. It can be a little annoying at times, but there are ways of preventing it happening. First of all you must have the correct elastic strengths. It is no use threading three sections with elastics such as number three, four and five, as these should be passed through two sections only. When you are fishing remember to lubricate your elastic thoroughly, as this dispels water from within the tip sections,

preventing the elastic from sticking to the insides of the pole or drip the lubricant into the tip. Pour quite a lot into your pole by removing the bung.

Another superb way of storing the collapsed top three is by removing the bung from the third section and pulling the elastic from the pole. Now wind the elastic onto a winder, lay this against the side of your third section and attach it to the section using an elastic band. When you come to fish you simply remove the winder and pull your telescopic top three apart and the elastic and bung will settle into the correct place.

Attaching strange floats

Q I would like to do some carp fishing using my pole and I have heard that a swivel dibber is one of the best floats for this. Could you please tell me how to attach it correctly?

A This is a very good question, as the swivel attached to the float is so small you cannot use an adaptor; neither can you use a couple of large shot to lock

▶ *To prevent swivel dibbers from moving along your mainline, thread the line through the swivel twice, then lock it in place with shot.*

the float in place, as they will sink the float.

Another problem I have found is when clipping the float in place using two ultra-small shot, say number 10s. You cannot squeeze them onto the line too tightly or they will damage the monofilament. If you squeeze them on lightly, the float may move along the line when playing a large fish.

There is a solution though: all you need to do is thread your mainline through the swivel twice. This forms a tight loop around the swivel's eye. Now you can clip on two small shot either side of the float. This is a method that will prevent your float moving anywhere. Then you can use your float to present either a bait at mid-depth, or on the bottom tight to marginal weeds or snags.

Fill in the cracks

Q Recently, while fishing my local canal a strong wind blew my pole

off its roller. It landed on a cobbled path causing two half-inch cracks along the centre of my eighth section. Will these cracks affect the strength and performance of my pole? If so, what can I do to cure the problem?

A There is a simple answer to this question and it is yes - the two

cracks will cause you problems in both performance and strength. Maybe they won't straight away, but given time they will open-up every time your pole flexes when used beyond the eighth section.

There are two ways of solving this problem, the first is to replace your number eight section altogether. This may cost you a fair amount, as the thicker the pole section, the more expensive they are.

The other alternative is to have your section repaired. I actually saw the results of a really skilful job at Angling '97. The results were absolutely fantastic, and a lot cheaper than a brand new pole section, too!

Keep the tip

Q I have just bought a new pole specifically for carp fishing. I would like to know if I can discard the tip section and just elasticate sections two, three and four instead?

A You can remove the tip section if you wish, but you may have a great deal of trouble trying to find a PTFE bush to fit the end of your number two section.

Personally I prefer keeping my tip section, even if it means there is only a few inches of it protruding. Now you are much more likely to find a bush to fit your cut-back tip section. This also makes your tip section stronger, as there is a doubled-up length of carbon where number one and number two sections meet.

If I were you I'd keep your number one section, even if it means there is only three or four inches remaining.

Making your own rigs

Q I've just started pole fishing and I would like to start making my own rigs. Some anglers say I should use styls, some say to use olivettes. What do you prefer, and why?

A Styls and olivettes are two different weights entirely. Styls are actually small cylindrical shots which are most commonly used in the same way as small split shot, whereas olivettes are pear-shaped weights which act as a bulk weight. I do not use styls anymore. They are fiddly little things which are a pain to get onto the line, and even more difficult to move once squeezed on, as they lock solid.

By far the best alternative is to use split shot instead. They can be moved up or down your mainline quite easily and if your float is over-shotted, they are easy to take off. But this is purely personal preference, you can use whatever you wish. I do use olivettes whenever I require a large bulk of weight for sinking my bait to the bottom or to combat powerful flows. Your line passes through the centre of the olivette which allows you to move them along the line whenever you wish.

Putting on weight

Q I have recently started making up my own pole rigs. I would like to know how much of the float's weight should be taken up by an olivette, and also, how far from the hook should the olivette be placed?

A The answer is that as a general rule, you should use the vast majority of weight in the olivette, with as few and as small dropper shot as possible underneath. The less droppers you use the less complicated your rig will be, and much more tangle-free into the bargain.

If I was rigging up a 0.6g float I would select a 0.5g olivette. The remaining 0.1g of weight would be taken up by either one, two or three dropper shot below. This is the general rule for fishing stillwaters, but for river work I would decrease the size of the olivette and use more, or larger dropper shot below it.

As a general rule I would position the olivette two thirds of the way down the mainline, with the shot below, but you must always be prepared to move the olivette at any stage during the session. For example, if you are catching well with the fish taking the bait as soon as it touches the bottom, why wait ages for the bait to drop through the water?

In this situation I would normally expect to move the olivette closer to the hook, so the bait takes less time to reach the bottom, and this way I'd catch fish much faster.

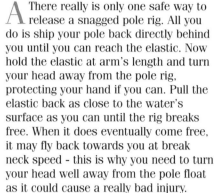

▲ *When targeting bottom feeders like bream or tench, slide your olivette closer to the hook.*

Pole-feeder facts

Q I have just started pole fishing, and I've been told there is a rig which involves both a float and a swimfeeder on the same line. Is this true and what are the benefits of this rig?

A Yes, this rig does exist and it can be absolutely deadly when the conditions are right. The rig consists of a bodied pole float followed by a simple paternoster link. To the shortest link, tie on either a groundbait or maggot feeder, to the longer link attach your hooklength and hook. This style of pole rig is best suited to running water, simply because you know your loosefed maggots or groundbait is sitting right over your hookbait. It allows you to drop your feeder in the same place time after time, building up your swim and at the same time ensuring the fish are tightly shoaled. The River Trent is a perfect venue to try this rig, but you could also give it a try at somewhere like Tetney Lock where anglers are often pegged very close together.

Therefore you need your feed to always be in the same place, and not drifting towards the angler next to you. Use a very light maggot feeder filled with red pinkies or squatts and a size 22 hook with a red maggot on the hook.

It may also be worthwhile trying breadpunch in a feeder with punch on the hook in winter for the larger roach.

Freeing snagged rigs

Q When I snag the bottom when using a pole I am at a loss as to what is the best and safest action to take. Can you help?

A There really is only one safe way to release a snagged pole rig. All you do is ship your pole back directly behind you until you can reach the elastic. Now hold the elastic at arm's length and turn your head away from the pole rig, protecting your hand if you can. Pull the elastic back as close to the water's surface as you can until the rig breaks free. When it does eventually come free, it may fly back towards you at break neck speed - this is why you need to turn your head well away from the pole float as it could cause a really bad injury.

If you can work the pole and elastic back until you reach the line you will have more chance of recovering the rig as your tugs will not be absorbed by the elastic. All the time remember to turn away from the rig while pulling, I cannot stress this enough!

Elastic problems

Q At the start of a session my elastic tension is fine - it slips back perfectly. After I have played a fish the elastic hangs from the pole tip. If I shake the pole, or pull the elastic it will normally slide back into the pole. What is wrong?

A It sounds as though you have set your pole elastic to the correct tension, but you are missing one vital aspect - you should always lubricate your pole before every single session. I cannot stress this fact enough, many pole anglers forget to lubricate their elastic and end up having all sorts of problems.

Before fishing you should pull your bung from you first, second or third section and drip a substantial quantity of lubricant straight down your top kit. This will saturate the outside of your elastic, lubricating it, and at the same time, eliminating any friction between your elastic and the PTFE bush at the tip of your pole. There are many different kinds of lubricant available, all

◄ *Use a lubricant before every session to cut down friction.*

of which perform brilliantly. I always use Preston Innovations' lubricant whenever I am pole fishing and that has never let me down yet.

Shotting problems

Q When I am pole fishing, the shots I use on my rigs tend to damage the line when I need to move them up or down. When I loosen them they usually drop off. Please could you help me!

A This can be a real problem, but there is a way to prevent this happening. First of all you need to use the right size and good quality shot.

English pole floats are very sensitive things which only need tiny shots down the line. There really is no need to use shots larger than number eights. If you do need a large bulk, then an olivette is far better. Your shot should either be number eights, nines, 10s, 11s, 12s or 13s. Opt for quality shot, like those made by Preston Innovations, Colmic or Maver, and don't squeeze them on too tightly or else this will damage your line.

A tip worth trying when making your own rigs is to attach all your shot at the end of your mainline. When all the necessary shot are attached, gently slide them one by one, 10 inches along the line. Now cut off the line where you attached the shot as it is damaged. The shot opens up slightly when you moved it, and will therefore move along your line easily whenever required.

Top kit queries

Q I don't really understand the term spare top fours, threes, twos and one. I know it refers to the section numbers, but why the need for the different ones? Why not fish top fours instead?

A The reason why anglers don't fish top fours at all times is because of the depth of venue they are fishing. Obviously, if you are breaking your pole down at the fourth section you will be swinging in about 15 feet of line. What happens when you are fishing a canal, and the depth is about five feet? You would need 10 feet of line between your float and pole tip to make up the extra line needed to swing to hand. This would make controlling your rig, shipping out and your overall presentation difficult.

So in this case the angler should disregard his third and fourth spare sections and just fish with a spare top two instead. Match anglers tend to buy a variety of spare top kit lengths purely for this reason as they fish a wide variety of venues having a wide variety of depths.

Which length is best?

Q My dad has just bought me a 12.5m Shimano Perfection pole. I am a complete beginner to pole fishing and would like to know how long I should use the pole to enable me to get used to it properly. Also, what is an ideal starter's elastic?

A Many people would agree that the best way to learn is to throw yourself in at the deep end – not literally though! You obviously want to become the next Bob Nudd, and to do so you must catch some fish or else the only thing you

A multitude of spare top kits allows Bob to fish plenty of different methods, putting more fish in the net.

Q&A Pole fishing browser

will be learning is how to hold a pole for long periods of time. I certainly wouldn't suggest fishing a pole for the first time at its longest as you will experience all manner of difficulties. I would suggest visiting a venue where you know there are plenty of small fish which can be caught fairly close to the bank, at around eight metres. This will give you a good idea of how to hold a pole correctly, how to place your rig into the swim, strike, play fish, land fish and ship out. If you take this advice I would suggest threading your pole with a number three or four elastic through two sections. Your rig should have an 0.10mm mainline coupled with a 0.08mm hooklength.

Which colour is best?

Q I have recently started pole fishing and I am unfamiliar with the different types of pole floats. Please could you give me a rough guide as to what colour float tips I should use in different types of weather. I find it hard to see dark coloured floats in dull weather conditions.

A You will find there are three main tip colours: yellow, red and black. All these are designed for use, not in different weather conditions, more in different light conditions.

Light, as it hits the water's surface, forms different reflections. Some will be bright blue, even a blinding white, and some reflections will be at the other end of the spectrum: brown and even black. These differently coloured reflections should determine which colour float tip you should use.

To help you decide, sit on your box and look out onto the water surface to where you will be fishing. Look closely and you will see coloured reflections. As a general rule, if the reflections are dark, select a yellow-tipped float. If the sun is high and there are no trees, buildings or hills on the horizon the water will tend to be quite bright. Under these circumstances you should select a float having a black tip. If the water's surface is rippled and there are a multitude of bright and dark reflections bouncing across

◄ Reflections on the water should determine your float tip colour.

◄ *Don't worry about the pole hitting the water unless you are fishing a clear, shallow venue.*

the water use a red tip.

It is always worth carrying a black permanent marker in your tackle box, because the light may change at any time during the day, so you may have to darken the tip to help you see bites.

How does it work?

Q I have recently asked my local tackle dealer for information on how to shot pole floats. He told me to use a Dosopiombo which doesn't float or sink. Could you please tell me why it doesn't float or sink and how to use it correctly?

A It's a bit technical, this one! Dosopiombos do not float or sink, because they have a neutral buoyancy. In other words, the Dosopiombo is constructed from a finely balanced mixture of buoyant material and material which sinks. This combination has been tuned perfectly, so when it is gently dropped into water it just 'hangs around' between the surface and the bottom.

To use a Dosopiombo simply place your pole float's stem into the locking device and place into a spaghetti jar or vase which is full of water. Now gently drop small shot onto the Dosopiombo's round lip until the float is dotted down correctly. Now retrieve the float, together with Dosopiombo and all the shot required to cock the float correctly. Attach the pole float to your choice of mainline and gently squeeze on your shot to form a rig.

Disturbing fish

Q I am a newcomer to the world of pole fishing and sometimes I get careless. While shipping the pole out I occasionally splash the water's surface. Will this disturb the fish?

A Under the majority of circumstances I do not think this does disturb the fish, in fact I have watched top French anglers fishing and they purposefully throw their poles onto the surface immediately before feeding balls of groundbait. This splashing initially scares the nearby fish, but the inquisitive ones soon turn around to inspect the noise as they think it could be food dropping onto the water.

I do try to keep the pole tip off the water as much as possible but in some circumstances, when fishing is at venues with high banks behind you, it is impossible to prevent. If you are fishing shallow, gin-clear venues I would take steps to prevent your pole from hitting the water, but if you are fishing coloured and deep venues you shouldn't worry about it at all.

Should I whip?

Q I am considering whipping approximately a quarter-of-an-inch of all the female joints of my pole. I believe it will help to keep the joints stiff and, at the same time, protect the ends from accidentally splitting. Do you think it is worth it?

A Whipping the ends of all your female joints certainly won't make your pole any stiffer, in fact it will make it slightly softer, simply because you will be adding weight throughout the pole, even though it is only a small amount. I honestly do not think it is advisable to whip the female sections at all, as most poles do come with already reinforced female sections anyway.

If I were you I'd just reinforce your male sections by inserting either Drennan Polemaster or Preston Innovations' joint aligners. These will help stop you crashing your joints together when building up the pole while fishing. Whipping the female sections only adds to your problems as the pole wouldn't be quite as smooth when you ship out or in, as there will be 'bumps' every 1.5 metres to deal with. Also, when you put your pole away at the end of a session the whipped joints may not slide inside the next largest section.

◄ *Bob's a fan of joint aligners.*

Will powergum help?

Q I have trouble setting the hook when using elastics between three and six. I have considered using a length of powergum instead of elastic as this would provide some backbone to set the hook. Is this an option? If not, how do I overcome the problem?

A For a start, powergum, in the circumstances you state certainly isn't an option. The only time I would advise using powergum is when fishing in places such as Ireland or Denmark, when you are faced with a feeding shoal of big roach or bream and need to catch them quickly.

I can think of two solutions to solve your problem. The first is to strike with a little more force. Strike directly upwards with a hard, but controlled action. This should set the hook into the fish, but if it does not, simply take out the elastic you are using and thread in another that is one grade stronger. Try using a number four elastic instead of a three and this should solve your problems.

Q&A Pole fishing browser

Bothered by tangles

Q I am new to pole fishing and would like you to solve my very irritating problem. When I ship out, my rig often becomes badly tangled. Please can you help, as this is really bothering me!

A Many pole fishing newcomers suffer this problem, but don't worry as there are ways of preventing this happening. First of all think about the shipping-out process. Are you rushing it? If you are there will be times when your pole tip bounces all over the place, ultimately flicking your rig around until the line wraps over the float and tangles. So the first lesson is to take it steady. You should also ship your pole out in a straight line – straight towards your fishing area. If your pole sways from left to right your mainline will snake across the water and this too could cause tangles. You should also look closely at the length of line between pole tip and float. If the distance is short, say about one foot or less, this could be the root of your problem. Always have at least two feet of line between pole tip and float which should eliminate tangles.

Never point your pole towards larger hooked fish.

What went wrong?

Q I recently saw a pole angler hook into a very large carp. The fish swam away from him, towards the centre of the lake. His pole was pointing directly towards the fish and disaster struck – the fish vanished with the angler's top three sections. Could he have done anything to prevent this?

A Yes, he could have avoided this problem and I hope to god he was using barbless hooks. The reason why the fish took his top three kit is probably because it wasn't secured correctly inside his fourth section. If his top three kit was all telescopic then the first weak spot along the pole will be the fourth section which will either be put-in or put-over. If the elastic bottomed out, as it obviously did, something else has to give, in this case his pole. This accident could have been prevented simply by using lighter hooklength lines which would have broken before the pole gave way, or he could have attempted to move the pole tip to the side instead of keeping it pointing directly at the fish. After all, you would never play a carp using a rod with the tip pointing directly at the fish would you?

Fancy a dual?

Q I have heard of pole anglers using two different strength elastics within the same top kit with a stronger elastic situated at the bung end. As I do not have the cash to buy any spare top kits as yet, do you think this is a good idea? Could you explain how it works, too?

A The system you talk about is from Preston Innovations and is called the Dual Elastication Bung. If you have only one top kit, then yes, this really is a great idea as it will help prevent bumping smaller fish when using strong elastics. The idea is great as you can use two different elastic

strengths providing the second elastic is twice the 'strength' of the first – two and four, or five and ten and so on. You must remember to have your weaker elastic at the bung end of the set-up, not the way you described. All other instructions are printed on the system's packaging.

Hooklength dilemma

Q I have been told never to put any shot on the hooklength because of line damage. If this is true, how long should I have an un-shotted hooklength when pole or whip fishing?

A Yes, you can place shot onto your hooklength. Sometimes it is neccessary to have a little weight on your hooklength in order to register bites correctly. I tend to use a hooklength around 12 inches long, as you will have seen from my three sessions out on the bank earlier in the book. But if I were missing bites, or I felt my presentation needed altering slightly then I would place a shot or two onto my hooklength. Of course, they wouldn't be large shot – they would be number 12 or 13, small enough that they do not really damage your fine lines. Make sure you do not crush them onto the line with all your might, of course! But really it is up to you whether you wish to place shot onto your hooklength or not. If you feel you'd rather not risk placing weight on this finer line, opt to fish a hooklength of around six inches long and make sure your final shot is placed on your mainline, but pushed tight to the loop. This will ensure both neat presentation and bite registration.

Floating poles

Q I recently visited a small carp lake and was surprised to see an angler fishing with his pole laying flat on the water. When I asked what he was doing he said that he was free-lining. Is this really a good method and how do you see the bites?

A This method has accounted for a lot of huge carp weights – so many, in fact, that some fishery owners have banned this method, simply because anglers fishing this method are catching

▶ *Accurate groundbaiting and loosefeeding will tempt fish away from far bank cover eventually.*

too many fish. Although it is a very productive way of fishing, it doesn't work all the time. You will only catch when freelining in this way during the warmer months when the fish are feeding well and come up-in-the-water. The method is extremely simple. Once the carp are feeding very freely near the surface, simply take off your rig and replace with a 18-inch length of strong line, say 0.15mm diameter, around 5lb breaking strain. Now tie on and bait your strong hook. Ship out to your feeding zone and lay your pole on the surface. Place the pole butt between your legs and continue feeding small amounts, at regular intervals. Aim to loosefeed every 20 seconds or so. Eventually the fish will rise up to your suspended bait and take it. Bites are unmissable, as the elastic will stretch from the tip and your pole will drag across the water.

A ledge too far

Q I am due to fish a match on a local canal which is one to 1.5 metres wider than the length of my pole. As most match-winning weights come from the far side, I would like to know if there is any rig or method I could use to help in these circumstances?

A This could be a little difficult, to say the least, but I can assure you, it won't be impossible. Obviously you will be at a disadvantage as there will be anglers fishing the same match who have poles which will reach the far bank. An alternative is to fish a very light insert waggler, say around 2BB at the most, but this method will work only on calm days when there isn't too much surface disturbance. Flicking your rig out from your pole tip would be a little difficult as you won't really have enough weight down the line to flick the rig out far enough. I'm afraid the only alternative is to either purchase an extension for your pole if there is one available, or to feed a little groundbait containing chopped worm as far as your pole reaches at the start of the session via a pole cup. Now loosefeed caster over this area in an attempt to draw the

fish from the far bank. I suggest using the same rig as you would use for the canal's central track, but dot it right down so you will easily spot even the tiniest of bites.

Deep water tangles

Q My local club water is over 30 feet deep in some places. During the colder months all the best catches come from this deeper area. When I fish here I always use a rig having a three gramme olivette, positioned four feet from the hook, coupled with six No12 droppers set shirt-button style in between. My hook is set four inches overdepth. Although I do catch, I often get tangled around the hooklength when using this rig. What exactly is it that I am doing wrong?

A I do not know whether you are tangling after a missed bite, or whether the rig is tangling as the olivette settles following shipping out. Whichever of these happens, though, I think the reason is going to be due to the shotting patten below your olivette. As a cure, I would suggest using different sized shot between your bulk and hook. Try the following for a good solution – a number 8 shot beneath the olivette, then two number 10s, followed by one number 13. This difference in weight down the line will push your baited hook through the water neatly; at the same time it will prevent any angles as it drops. You may find that you have to alter the size of shot to ensure the float sits correctly in the water, replacing your number 10s with number 11s, instead.

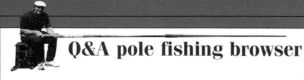

Q&A pole fishing browser

Which roller is your favourite?

Q My question regards pole rollers. Which pole roller do you prefer and why? Which is best – vee-shaped rollers, square versions having a single roller, or square ones having a double bottom roller?

A I much prefer using square versions having a 90 degree hinge between the base roller or rollers and the two smaller side rollers. These, I have found, are far better in strong winds. I have to admit that vee-shaped pole rollers are far better for speed fishing, where you need to whiz the pole through the rollers, but they do have their limitations. The last time I used one was at a match at Holme Pierrepont. It was extremely windy at the time and when I pushed my pole into the rollers, the pole sections travelled up the roller's side until it bounced off, landing on hard concrete. You can imagine what happened next! I actually use two different styles, the Browning free-standing pole roller and the Rolls-Royce of pole rollers, the Boss version. This model features a double base roller and is a magnificent piece of engineering. They aren't cheap, but Boss rollers are lightweight, fold away neatly and will last you a long, long time.

Storing tele top threes

Q I am new to pole fishing and although I enjoy it very much, I seem to struggle putting my pole away after each session. The telescopic top three, which are all elasticated, are very hard to push into each other. Is this because of the elastic, or am I doing something wrong?

A It can be extremely difficult to push an elasticated telescopic top three together – you have to be extremely careful to avoid trapping the elastic and not to rub the section ends along the elastic as this will surely damage it. I do not believe there is a simple way to do this, but I can offer an easy alternative.

At the end of your session simply remove the bung from your third section and slacken all the telescopic joints. Now hold the elastic bung alongside a large winder and wind on all the elastic until you finally draw the tip section from sections two and three. Now wrap an elastic band around the bung, winder and tip section and store in a seperate container or rod tube. All you have to do to set the telescopic top three up again is to drop the tip section through your second and third section and unravel your elastic. Pull the top three tight and your bung should slide into position.

Tangled whip rigs

Q When I cast with my whip the rig always seems to tangle. My friend tells me it is because of the way I have set my rigs up. They have split shot throughout – my friend says use rigs with an olivette. Is he right? If not, can you tell me where I am going wrong?

A I would think you are using a series of split shot set shirt-button style down the rig. This could be the root of your problem, particularly if you are casting the rig underarm. It is always

best to cast a rig of this kind overarm, as your rig will land in a straight line ahead. If you cast with an underarm flick, change your rig to suit. I suggest pulling the majority of the shot together to form a bulk. This should be placed just above your hooklength, at around one third of the water's depth. Push a couple of dropper shot between the bulk and your hook to allow a steady, natural fall of your hookbait and good bite registration. You could use an olivette rig instead, as they are fine for whip fishing, but a bulk of split shot can be separated along the mainline for an on-the-drop rig. Remember, if you are using such a rig you must cast with an overhead flick; if you are fishing a bulk rig, cast with an underarm flick.

Submerged tips

Q Would you ever advise sinking the pole tip when fishing and if so, under what conditions does this have its advantages?

A Yes, I certainly would advise sinking your pole tip, but only during adverse conditions, namely when it is so windy that your pole tip is being pulled

◀ *Bob much prefers using a square based, free-standing roller whenever pole fishing.*

all over the place, ultimately pulling your float off line and generally making a mess of your presentation. Sinking your pole tip is a great way to ensure that your rig is settled in these conditions. It's also worthwhile sinking the tip and line when whip fishing, often more so than pole fishing. Don't sink your pole tip too far under the water, as you could break the tip sections when striking directly up through the water. You need only sink the pole tip a few centimetres for it to pull the line between pole tip and float under the water.

Should I step-up?

Q **I use number three elastic for most stillwater roach fishing. I now wish to move onto my local River Trent. Do I need to step up elastic for this river to combat both the flow and tactics?**

A Yes, you need to step up your elastic, using a number 4, 5 or even a 6 through two sections. The reason why is simple. As you are fishing a flowing venue your rigs will be different. You should use either a body up or a round bodied float, which may require one, two, three or even four grammes to cock it correctly. This is because you need to get your bait down to the required depth. If you continue to use lightweight

stillwater style rigs your bait will just be pushed along with the flow. A stronger elastic not only provides you with a better strike, but also more control over hooked fish in strong flowing water.

Which float is best?

Q **As a newcomer to pole fishing I do not fully understand the different styles of pole floats. Which shape of float is best for rivers?**

A The answer to this question depends entirely on the river's condition. If it is flowing hard you need to adopt a different shape of float to a river that is running steady, or virtually at a standstill. For those venues which do flow try investing in a few round bodied floats. These ride the water well and can be held back against the flow when you wish your bait to flutter up from the river bottom. The pronounced shoulder of the float keeps it stable as you tighten up the line from pole tip to float. Also bear in mind the flow strength. If the river is flowing really hard use a large pole float which is capable of carrying two, three or even four grammes of weight to cock it correctly. This extra weight helps get your bait down to the feeding fish below. On calmer rivers, which do not flow too hard, you could

adopt the same style of float, but only 0.75 or one gramme in weight. If you are fishing off the bottom and allowing your bait to travel with the flow you could select a slightly more delicate float with a less prominent body shape. Try a slim float or one which has a slender body.

Can I fish a stick?

Q **Is it possible to fish a stick float when pole fishing? If so, how should I go about it?**

A Yes, it is possible, and believe me on its day this method can be a killer. Adopt the same shotting pattern you would use when stick float fishing with a rod and running line, but you must use a lighter stick float. In fact there are specially designed floats for this purpose, often called pole sticks, which are extremely lightweight and small. Avoid thick wire stemmed stick floats - the extra weight incorporated in the stem is unnecessary as you will ship the rig out as opposed to cast it out. You must also use a longer length of line between pole tip and float in order to trot the rig through the swim, but always keep this line fairly tight so you can connect with bites. It's a great method as you can present a bait at the length of your pole perfectly. Give it a try!

▲ *Use body-up floats in fast-flowing water or when you may need to hold back.*

▲ *Purpose-made pole sticks like these are great items for flowing venues.*

▲ *Slightly slimmer pole floats are best for use in slow-moving venues or stillwaters.*

Jargon-buster

You may think you know it all, but just in case you don't, here's a brief explanation of some of pole fishing's key items

All-through action
If a rod or pole is capable of bending throughout its length it is described as having an all-through action. It is a characteristic that is typical of thicker-walled poles, such as those designed for carp fishing. Bending through the whole length is designed to ease loads such as those caused by the surging thrusts of hard-fighting carp.

Baitwaiter
A simple, lightweight accessory that allows you to position bait directly alongside your seat. Use one if possible, as by doing so, you'll no longer have to bend down to get your loosefeed. With practice you'll be able to load your catapult without even having to take your eyes off the float.

Barbless hook
A type of hook that makes the difficult process of unhooking carp easier. Carp are fish that fight extremely well, often so well that they smash the hooklength, even the mainline. If this happens when using barbed

hooks, the fish will have the hook buried inside its mouth for the rest of its days. With a barbless hook, the story is very different, as it will eventually fall from the fish's mouth, causing no serious damage. These are important factors that have led to a ban on barbed hooks by most small carp fisheries.

Bung
A cylindrical or circular plastic device onto which elastic is tied. They fit into either sections one, two or three of your pole and hold the elastic in place.

Connector
A tiny plastic attachment which is permanently tied to the end of your elastic. Connectors allow a speedy attachment of pole rigs via a small loop in the end of the rig's mainline.

Diamond eye threader
A strong weaved length of stainless steel wire having a snake-like head. It is used to thread elastic through pole sections.

Dust shot
This is a catch-all group name for the smallest sizes of shot. They are sold as No10, No11, No12 and No13. The name originated as the shot is so fine that it resembles particles of dust.

Extension
Another 1 or 1.5 metres of pole which attaches to the end section to add extra length. Some pricey poles can extend up to 16 metres in length.

Line
Two types of fishing line are generally available, normal-strength reel line and high-tech pole line. High-tech is the best choice for pole fishing as such line has a ultra-fine diameter, plus a high breaking strain. Pre-stretching during manufacture gives such line almost double the breaking strain of an equivalent standard line. For example, a typical 0.14mm normal line has a breaking strain around the 2.1lb mark; the same diameter high-tech line will not snap before a pull of about 4lb is applied.

◄ The perfect setup for a successful haul of fish at the riverside. Bob lays out all his equipment 'just so', with everything to hand, ready for action at a moment's notice.

▲ *Winders, hemp and a good catch – basis of a good session's fishing for Bob.*

Liquid pellet

A great feed inducer that can drive carp into a thrashing frenzy of greed. It is basically the same oily, fishy additive which is sprayed onto trout pellets to make them more attractive to fish.

Lubricant

An essential item for pole fishing. Used to keep the elastic from sticking in the pole sections.

Olivettes

Specially moulded weights, which provide bulk in a neat, compact package. Olivettes can be either threaded onto the line or attached with small strips of silicone tubing. Olivettes are easy to use as they normally come in packets with individual weights marked on. An olivette's purpose is to provide the weight necessary to get your bait down to the bottom as quickly as possible. Another type of weight that can be used is the styl, a cylindrical weight which clasps onto the line.

Pole anchors

Small silicone links having a loop on one end, and a moulded hook at the other. They are used to connect the rig line to the pole winder when not in use. They are a vital item as, by hooking onto the end of your pole rig and to a hook on your winder, they keep your rig under tension and secure on your winder.

PTFE bush

A lightweight but strong plastic attachment that, when in place on the end of your pole, prevents elastic from rubbing against sharp carbon. There are two versions, internal and external. Bob prefers internal ones, as they are a lot neater, slipping inside the tip section and do not obstruct line or elastic. External bushes simply slide over the tip section, and are best used with super-strength elastics. They can be distracting to the eye, though, which may make the difference between getting a bite and missing it.

Put-in joints

Poles with put-in joint sections have the larger section slipping over the next smallest section.

Put-over joints

Poles having put-over joints have the larger section sliding into the next smaller section.

Rig rest

Another simple (and cheap, at about £5) accessory. It is a simple roost that is perfect for keeping extra top kits off the ground and out of harm's way. Bob always keeps his rig rests quite low in order to stop top kits blowing around too much in strong winds.

Silicone tubing

Normally available in packs of three different diameters. The tubing is used to hold the float tightly on the rig line and should be attached only on the float's stem.

Taper

The gradual pole diameter decrease over its length, from butt to tip section. A fast taper is typical of a 'roach pole', in which the decrease in section diameters is quite significant, making for lightness and a definite 'tip action', just right for playing these smaller fish.

Top three kits

The top three thinnest pole sections. They are often bought and fitted with different strength elastic to provide a spare when required.

Walls

The sides of the pole section. Thin-walled poles are generally lighter, but are also weaker and more prone to damage and breakages. All-round poles generally have thicker walls, which makes them stronger, though heavier than competition poles. All-rounders are also designed to be a little more forgiving, with more bending capacity in the top few sections – allowing you to tackle larger fish with some confidence. If you are a carp addict, then go for a specialist carp pole, with slight taper for stronger tip sections.

CALL FREE ON 0800 0180 371 AND SAVE UP TO 25% ON YOUR FAVOURITE ANGLING MAGAZINES...

Angling PLUS

If you want to catch more and catch faster in matches make sure you're getting *Angling Plus* for the latest tactics, techniques and strategies. There's more advice from Bob Nudd and many of the sport's other leading names, plus all the talk, news, previews, analysis, coverage and gear reviews, to help you win!

SAVE 15% Subscribe now for one year and receive 12 issues at £25.50 (normal price £30.00)

SAVE 25% Subscribe for two years and receive 24 issues at £45.00 (normal price £60.00)

Subscribe today and have your magazine/s delivered direct to your door, free of postage and packaging charges. Satisfaction guaranteed or your money back

ORDER BY FREEPOST

Simply select your chosen payment method and send your completed coupon to: EMAP Angling Publications, Angling Subscriptions Department, FREEPOST (MID 06119), Leicester LE87 4EM
If you prefer not to cut your book a photocopy is acceptable.

☎ OR FREEPHONE 0800 0180 371

Please quote "PJ24" for Improve Your Coarse Fishing and "PX1A" for Angling Plus when ordering. Please state if you currently subscribe. Credit card hotline open 8.30am to 9.00pm weekdays, 10.00am to 4.00pm weekends. Queries: please call 01858 468888 8.30am to 9.00pm weekdays only.

FOR LOTS MORE BOB NUDD AND ADVICE ON POLES...

IMPROVE YOUR COARSE FISHING

MARCH 1998 £2.10

Improve your angling technique and methods with Britain's best-selling angling magazine. Written by a team of experts, including Bob Nudd and television's John Wilson, Improve Your Coarse Fishing is THE magazine that shows you how its done!

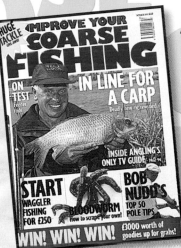

SAVE 15% Subscribe now for one year and receive 12 issues at £23.00 (normal price £27.00)

SAVE 25% Subscribe for two years and receive 24 issues at £40.50 (normal price £54.00)

John Wilson All Rounder

The Perfect Pole Peg

SUBSCRIPTION ORDER FORM

I would like to subscribe to *Improve Your Coarse Fishing* magazine. (PJ24)
- ☐ £23.00 for 12 issues (total one year saving £4.00) — J2I
- ☐ £40.50 for 24 issues (total two years saving £9.50) — J2J

I would like to subscribe to *Angling Plus* magazine. (PX1A)
- ☐ £25.50 for 12 issues (total one year saving £4.50) — X1W
- ☐ £45.00 for 24 issues (total two years saving £15.00) — X1X

YOUR DETAILS

Title (Mr/Mrs/Miss/Ms) _____ Full name _____

Address _____

Postcode _____ Daytime Tel No. _____

E-mail _____

DETAILS OF PAYER (If paying for a friend or relative)

Title (Mr/Mrs/Miss/Ms) _____ Full name _____

Address _____

Postcode _____ Daytime Tel No. _____

E-mail _____

SELECT ONE PAYMENT METHOD

1. PAY BY CREDIT CARD

Please debit £............ ....from my Access/Visa/Amex/Diners Card no.

☐☐☐☐ ☐☐☐☐ ☐☐☐☐ ☐☐☐☐

Expiry Date _____

Signature _____

Today's date _____

2. PAY BY CHEQUE/POSTAL ORDER

I enclose a cheque/postal order for £........ made payable to: **Emap Pursuit Publishing Limited**

CURRENT SUBSCRIBERS

You can renew your subscription/s using this offer ☐ Yes, I wish to renew my subscription to Improve Your Coarse Fishing/Angling Plus (delete as appropriate) using this offer. My subscriber number is (if known)..

We may share information about you with our parent company, EMAP Plc, and our sister companies in the EMAP Group and also third parties where we feel their services may be of interest to you. If you do not wish your details to be passed on to these third parties, please tick this box ☐
I am over 18 ☐

Offer closes 31st December 1999 and is limited to the UK only. Overseas prices available upon request by calling 0(+44) 01858 468888 Prices shown based on 1998 subscription rates

NOW POST THIS COUPON TODAY!

Tailpiece

That's it, then – if you've read the book thoroughly, you should know pretty well as much as me about the satisfying art of pole fishing. Experience is another thing altogether, of course, but for that you simply need enthusiasm and lots of lovely time by the water!
Tight lines and great pole fishing!

Bob Nudd